The
L.I.G.H.T.
Seminar

Living in the Gifts of the Holy Trinity

The L.I.G.H.T. Seminar

Living in the Gifts of the Holy Trinity

A Guide for Catholics and others
wanting to use the gifts of the Holy Spirit in everyday life.

Deacon
Michael Wesley

Foreword by Fr. Bob Hogan, BBD

outskirts
press

Author Endorsements

Thank you, Deacon Mike, for this wonderful, life changing seminar. - Joe Cieszinski: *Author of LOAVES AND FISHES – JESUS AND THE FEEDING OF THE MULTITUDES.*"

Deacon Mike offers a guide for those seeking divine gifts of the Holy Spirit. Included are gifts of holiness, gifts of power, gifts of service and others. He grounds out the reality of how to use these gifts in daily living and overcoming obstacles to using them. I am on fire just re-reading it again.. ---Mary Quinalty, Author *of Mountaintop Milagro*

Deacon Michael gives practical guidance and examples in how to become more open to the working of the Holy Spirit, and how to overcome obstacles to living fully in the Spirit. ... He explains the individual gifts and helps us to see their value for our lives. Fr. Bob Hogan, BBD. *(Author of Celebrating a Charismatic Jubilee)*

Dedication Page

This book is dedicated to the greater glory of God and to my wife, Kathy, who is one of God's greatest gifts to me.

"Glory be to him whose power, working in us, can do infinitely more than we can ask or imagine."

—Ephesians 3:20–21, The Jerusalem Bible

Acknowledgements

I would like to thank the following people for their help in the production of this book: Fr. Bob Hogan, BBD, Sr. Miriam Grady, DLJC, Mary Quinalty, Joseph Cieszinski, MTS, Andrew Ortiz, Art Garcia, Ethel Garcia, Nestor and Nellie Baca, Vincent Montoya, Deacon Frank Smith, Kathy Wesley, Marcella Gibson, Betty Braswell, Jane Zingelman, Patricia Gutierrez, and John Fidel (of happy memory).

Table of Contents

Foreword

In the L.I.G.H.T Seminar (Living in the Gifts of the Holy Trinity) Deacon Michael R. Wesley seeks to help Catholics grow in their understanding of the Holy Spirit and the gifts of the Spirit. He has known many Catholics who have had an experience of spiritual renewal in their lives through movements like the ACTS retreat, Cursillo, RCIA, youth retreats, etc. Their experience is similar to those who have gone through a Life in the Spirit Seminar through Charismatic Renewal groups. Their faith is more alive, and they have a greater desire to share their faith with others.

Often what is missing is an understanding of how to allow the Holy Spirit to work in one's life for service and evangelization through the gifts of the Spirit ("charisms" is the word in Greek used in the New Testament that is translated as "gifts of the Spirit").

Deacon Michael explains both the gifts of the Spirit found in Isaiah 11 and the charismatic gifts found in the New Testament. The seven gifts of the Spirit found in Isaiah 11 are more commonly known and taught in the Catholic Church. Building on the teaching of the Second Vatican Council, all the popes since the Council have emphasized the importance of refocusing on the importance of the charismatic gifts, which commonly have not been explained well in the Catholic teaching.

This book will help you to understand and experience both the Isaiah 11 gifts and the charismatic gifts. Deacon Michael gives practical guidance and examples in how to become more open to the working of the Holy Spirit, and how to overcome obstacles to living fully in the Spirit. He explains the individual gifts and helps us see their value for our lives. I have often said in my teaching that if God has given you a responsibility or "calling," you should seek the spiritual empowerment (spiritual gifts) that will allow God to work through you to complete your God-given responsibility or "calling." This book is a wonderful aid that can enable us to allow the Holy Spirit to accomplish God's work in our lives.

—Fr. Bob Hogan. BBD

Fr. Bob has taught Theology at two Catholic Universities. He is the author of a book on the charismatic dimension of the Church and charismatic renewal, Celebrating a Charismatic Jubilee. *He is the former chairperson of the National Service Committee for Catholic Charismatic Renewal in the USA. He is presently a member of CHARIS National Service of Communion USA, which is the USA branch of the new structure that Pope Francis has organized for Catholic Charismatic Renewal throughout the world.*

A LIGHT Apology

Although we do have a LIGHT seminar this is not a how-to book on presenting one. Those involved with setting up a seminar will usually have prior experience working a Life in the Spirit Seminar or a similar retreat or group activity. For those wanting more information you can send an email to lightseminar1@gmail.com. I may eventually come up with a manual.

For those wanting to host a one-day LIGHT seminar I have provided a tentative schedule on the next page. This is just one option. The seminar can also be done over several days or over the internet. Suggested questions can be found at the end of most of the chapters in this book. These can be used for personal reflection or group discussion. Some of these can be eliminated in a seminar or group activity to expand the time for the teachings.

The teachings presented in this guide are not intended to replace the guidance of the Holy Spirit, nor the teacher's own knowledge or experience. They are meant to provide a theological foundation for the topics covered in the L.I.G.H.T. seminar. After all, one can grow in the gifts of the Holy Spirit without ever attending a L.I.G.H.T. seminar. However, these teachings could be used as a springboard to guide the presenters in developing their own teaching.

What is most important in receiving the gifts of the Holy Spirit is an open heart and a desire to serve God as fully as possible.

Suggested Schedule for the
One-Day LIGHT Seminar

Registration	8:30–9:00
Welcoming	9:00–9:20
The Gifts Are for Everyone	9:20–9:45
The Seven Gifts of the Holy Spirit	9:45–10:10
Discussion/Break	10:10–10:20
Experiencing the Word Gifts in Everyday Life	10:20–10:45
Experiencing the Gifts of Power in Everyday Life	10:45–11:10
Discussion /Break	11:10–11:25
Experiencing the Gifts of Revelation	11:25–11:50
Lunch	11:50–12:30
Experiencing the Gifts of Service in Everyday Life	12:30–12:55
Experiencing the Gifts of Ephesians 4:11:	12:55–1:20
Break/Discussion	1:20–1:30
Obstacles to Living the Spirit-Filled Life	1:30–1:55
Prayer of Forgiveness	1:55-2:15
Break/Discussion	2:15-2:25
Prayer for Discovering the Gifts	2:25-2:50
Growing in the Spirit-Filled Life	2:50-3:15
Spiritual Warfare	3:15-3:40
Concluding Remarks/Final Prayer	3:40-4: 00

CHAPTER 1

What the Heck is the LIGHT Seminar?

The word "LIGHT" is an acronym for Living in the Gifts of the Holy Trinity. The purpose of the seminar is to acquaint Catholics and others with the gifts of the Holy Spirit. I say "others" because the seminar might also be of interest to non-Catholics. I mention "Catholics" specifically, though, because there are many Catholics today who are on fire with their experience of God's presence and his love who know very little (if anything at all) about many of the gifts of the Holy Spirit.

Through movements such as the ACTS retreat, Cursillo, RCIA, and youth retreats, as well as just through their own spiritual growth, many Catholics have experienced the fire of the Holy Spirit! And what this fire of the Holy Spirit has created within them is a thirst to share their faith with others. They are on fire with their love for the Church, their love for Jesus

Christ, and their hunger to share this Good News with others!

This is all very good because it is through witnessing the power of the Holy Spirit that our secular world is going to be drawn to God. And some of the tools God has given us to display his power are the gifts of the Holy Spirit.

I began to learn about the gifts of the Holy Spirit in April of 1971 through the Catholic Charismatic Renewal.[1] I'll elaborate on this more in the next chapter. But it was through the Catholic Charismatic Renewal that I experienced this awareness of God's presence, his love for me, and a personal relationship with Jesus Christ. It was in the Renewal that I experienced the "baptism in the Holy Spirit."[2]

---

1   The word "charismatic" comes from the Greek word "charis," meaning "gift." The designation "charismatic" is given to someone who believes that the charismatic gifts of the Holy Spirit (see 1 Corinthians 12:6–10, Romans 12:6–8, Ephesians 4:11–12) are still active in the church today. Reference to the charismatic dimension of the Church is mentioned in Lumen Gentium 4, 7, 12, 30–31.

2   The term "baptism in the Holy Spirit" refers to an experience of the empowerment of the Holy Spirit in the life of a Christian. In all four gospels John the Baptist says the Messiah will "baptize in the Spirit." In Acts 1:5 the apostles are told that in a few days thy will be "baptized in the Holy Spirit."

Many Catholics have also received the baptism in the Holy Spirit outside of the Charismatic Renewal. It would have been seen more as a conversion experience than

> One need not be a practicing member of the Charismatic Renewal to receive the baptism in the Holy Spirit.

anything else, although that's exactly what the baptism in the Holy Spirit is. This is a very important point. One need not be a practicing member of the Catholic Charismatic Renewal to receive the baptism in the Holy Spirit.

One of the benefits of receiving the baptism in the Holy Spirit in the Charismatic Renewal, though, is the emphasis that's placed on the gifts of the Holy Spirit. It is a way of learning what the gifts of the Holy Spirit are and how God works through them.

The Pajama Story

Have you ever had what you thought was a good idea, but you left one important element out? This happened to me when I was nine years old. Waking up in the wee hours of the morning I saw my dad asleep on the couch with the television on. The program that he had been watching was *Joan of Arc* starring Ingrid

Bergman. Not being allowed to watch television that late at night, I saw this as an adventure. I sat on the floor and watched the remainder of *Joan of Arc*.

I was impressed by the little I saw of it and decided that I wanted to be a saint. The only problem was I had no idea how I was going to do this. After watching the story of St. Joan of Arc, though, the idea came to me that one of the ways I could become a saint was by dressing like one. I noticed that the attire worn by St. Joan of Arc in the movie looked a lot like my pajamas.

So, I decided that if I wore my pajamas to school every day I would become a saint. It seems like a silly idea now, but at the time it made a lot of sense. I knew my mom was not going to let me wear my pajamas to school, though, even if it was to make me a saint. So I devised a scheme where I'd put my pajamas on under my school uniform, change clothes before getting to school, and change into my regular clothes before returning home.

At the time it seemed like a flawless idea. What I failed to consider, though, is where was I going to change my clothes on the way to school, and where was I going to keep them all day long? And it never even occurred to me that the nuns were not going to let me spend the day at school in my pajamas. My plan had left out some very important parts.

So, the next day I tried sneaking out of the house with my saintly looking pajamas under my school uniform. But as I said goodbye to my mom she caught sight of the bulge underneath my corduroy pants. Checking inside my pants and seeing the pajamas she ordered me to take them off and never do that again! She probably thought I was bordering insanity.

The reason I'm sharing this story is because the gifts of the Holy Spirit are often taught while leaving out some very important parts: *the charismatic gifts of the Holy Spirit.* It is for this reason I decided to develop the L.I.G.H.T. seminar. It is to be a means of acquainting and equipping Catholics outside of the Charismatic Renewal with some of the additional tools God has given them for ministry. My belief is that the Pentecostal fire will burn even brighter as these zealous Catholics begin to discover and use all the gifts of the Holy Spirit.

In John 14:12 Jesus told his disciples, "Amen, amen, I say to you, whoever believes in me will do the works that I do, and will do greater ones than these, because I am going to the Father" (The New American Bible). In this way, Jesus was telling his apostles [and us] that we are to continue ministering in the same way he did: through teaching, healing, forgiving, performing miracles, giving unconditional love, and practicing Christian unity.

The way we do this is by following Jesus's teachings and the utilization of the gifts of the Holy Spirit. In John 10b–11 Jesus said, "The Father who dwells in me

> Our primary ministry as Catholic/Christians is not just to serve, but to bring Jesus's presence to a world that is longing to meet him.

is doing his works. Believe me that I am in the Father and the Father is in me, or else, believe because of the works themselves" (NAB).

The gifts of the Holy Spirit are the works of Jesus flowing through us. We should be able to tell people, "If you don't believe me because of my words, believe because of the works that you see flowing through me."

My Reintroduction to the Holy Spirit

I think I was in third grade when I initially became interested in the Holy Spirit. At the time I was attending a Catholic School in southern California. One day our teacher taught us about the day of Pentecost.

She told us that the Holy Spirit had come down upon the early believers and empowered them with such courage and love that many gladly gave their lives for God. They were filled with a tremendous joy, and their love for each other radiated from their hearts. There were miracles, healings, and the grace of the Holy Spirit abounded among them!

I remember getting excited about it and thinking, "Wow, this is really neat! Maybe this is something I can experience too!" But then the teacher completely popped my bubble when she said, "But, of course, this doesn't happen anymore." Now, that may not be exactly what she meant or perhaps even what she said, but that's how I remember it. In any case, it left me believing that the Pentecostal experience was for an era long past.

When I was nineteen years old, I attended a branch of Eastern New Mexico University in Roswell. I had completely left my Catholic roots by this time because I didn't see the Church having any of the answers I was seeking for.

During my second semester I was introduced to a young man (I'll call him Steve) who was also nineteen. At first, we seemed to have a lot in common: an interest in philosophy, contemporary music, and social issues. So, when he asked to meet with me that evening to continue our discussion, it seemed like a good idea.

I thought we were going to talk about philosophy, drugs, music, girls, and the important things in life. When we met that evening, there was an older guy with Steve who must have been at least in his thirties. (I'll call him Frank.) I wondered what the heck he was doing there! I eventually discovered that Frank was a Baptist charismatic Christian and Steve was a Catholic charismatic Christian.

Their initial intention was simply to share Jesus with me. Friends may have told them I was living a wild, senseless lifestyle and needed Jesus in my life. I'm not sure why they chose to take me under their wings, but there I was arguing with Steve about the pros and cons of Christianity. He seemed to have a better grasp of information than I did, but I was holding my own pretty well with him. But then Frank brought out the big guns!

He looked over at me and said, "Mike, there's a tape I want to play for you." He played a reel-to-reel recording of people sharing about an experience they had of something called the baptism in the Holy Spirit. They were filled with a tremendous awareness of God's love.

Peace and joy radiated from their hearts, and each of them had received various gifts of the Holy Spirit!

As I listened to the tape I was suddenly brought back to third grade when I was told that Pentecost was a thing of the past. Now I was being told that Pentecost was still very much alive! The only way Frank could have known the significance that tape would have for me was by the Holy Spirit. All I wanted to know now was how I could experience the baptism in the Holy Spirit.

We talked more about having a personal relationship with Jesus Christ and the Spirit-filled life. Now I was ready to listen. That night outside my dormitory room I asked Jesus Christ to come into my heart and be the Lord of my life. There were no fireworks or bubbly feelings of joy, but there was a quiet peace that let me know God had heard my prayer.

Shortly after that I purchased my first Bible. In my dormitory room that night I randomly opened the Bible and my eyes fell on these words: "I know the plans I have in mind for you—it is Yahweh who speaks—plans for peace, not disaster, reserving a future full of hope for you" (Jeremiah 29:11–12, JB).

This was a very significant passage for me because a week before I had concluded that I had no hope in life. I had previously moved in with some friends off campus; we called ourselves freaks. Consequently, I was flunking most of my classes, and seemed to be making the same mistakes I always had. I wasn't happy, had not been for a while, and it seemed like I never would be.

I decided that my lot in life was to be a loser; there was nothing that could change that. But now God was telling me I had a future full of hope? Only the Holy Spirit could have opened the Bible to the exact passage I needed to read. This doesn't happen all the time, but on this particular instance I do believe it was the power of the Holy Spirit turning those pages of scripture. This gave me an incredible sense of peace and joy.

Since then I have been very active in the Catholic Charismatic Renewal. Through the Renewal, I have experienced a personal relationship with Jesus Christ, an awareness of God's love for me, a desire to share Jesus with others, and several of the charismatic gifts of the Holy Spirit. I went from not wanting anything to do with the Church to becoming an ordained deacon. And perhaps the greatest gift I received from this was that I went from having no hope at all to being filled full of hope!

Aside from the charismatic gifts, though, what I experienced wasn't much different from what others outside of the Charismatic Renewal have experienced—that is, except for a knowledge and use of the gifts of the Holy Spirit. That's what encouraged me to start the L.I.G.H.T. seminar. I wanted to provide a means for on-fire Catholics not directly involved with the Renewal to learn about the charismatic gifts of the Holy Spirit. I wondered why the charismatic gifts of the Holy Spirit wouldn't be for them too.

> This book is for anyone who has a hunger and thirst to serve God through the gifts of the Holy Spirit.

The LIGHT Seminar is not an exhaustive teaching on the gifts of the Holy Spirit. There are more detailed descriptions of the gifts that have been given by others. The purpose of this book is simply to present what some of the gifts are and how they can be used in everyday life.

Our challenge is to be opened to receiving all the gifts of the Holy Spirit God wants us to have. Why would we not want to receive a gift God wants us to have? Perhaps it's because we don't know what the gifts are and how God can use us through them. As you read through the L.I.G.H.T. seminar pray for the grace to be open to those gifts God may want you to have.

The gifts of the Holy Spirit, including the charismatic gifts, aren't just for those in the Catholic Charismatic Renewal. They are for every Catholic and every Christian wanting to be a disciple of Jesus Christ.

CHAPTER 2

The Gifts of the Holy Spirit Are for Everyone!

The twentieth century was an era of many theological changes and surprises in the Roman Catholic Church. One of these was the Second Vatican Council that began on October 11, 1962. A second surprise was the spontaneous generation of what came to be called the Catholic Charismatic Renewal.

What was surprising about these two events was their positive focus on the laity. This was a definite change from what the Church's attitude on the laity had been since the late Middle Ages, especially following the Council of Trent in the sixteenth century.

For about five hundred years the theological view of the Catholic Church was what Avery Dulles called, the "Institutional Model."[3] What was important in this model was the Church functioning as an institution. The active participants in this ecclesial machinery were the clergy and religious. They were responsible to teach, sanctify and govern while the laity were responsible to be taught, to be sanctified, and to be governed.

An example of how the hierarchy viewed its relationship with the laity can be seen in this quote from Saint Pope Pius X:

> The Church is essentially an *unequal* society, that is, a society comprising two categories of persons, the Pastors and the flock . . . So distinct are these categories that with the pastoral body only rests the necessary right and authority for promoting the end of the society and directing all its members toward that end; the one duty of the multitude is to allow themselves to be led, and, like a docile flock, to follow the Pastors.[4]

---

3   More information about the institutional model of the Church can be found in chapter two of the book, *Models of the Church*, by Avery Dulles.

4   Pope Pius X, *Vehementer Nos: On the French Law of Separation*, #8 (1906).

This view of the laity was to change with the Second Vatican Council. In the Decree on the Apostolate of Lay people we're told:

> The Holy Spirit sanctifies the People of God through the ministry and the sacraments. However, for the exercise of the apostolate he gives the faithful special gifts besides (cf. 1 Cor. 12:7), "allotting them to each one as he wills" (1 Cor. 12:11), so that each and all, putting at the service of others the grace received may be "as good stewards of God's varied gifts" (1 Pet. 4:10), for the building up of the whole body in charity (cf. Eph 4:16). From the reception of these charisms, even the most ordinary ones, there arises for each of the faithful the right and duty of exercising them in the Church and in the world for the good of men and the development of the Church, in exercising them in the freedom of the Holy Spirit who breathes where he wills" (Jn. 3:8).[5]

This new view focused on the power of the Holy Spirit working through the laity as well as the hierarchy, and

---

5   Austin Flannery, ed., *Vatican Council II, The Conciliar and Postconciliar Documents.* (Collegeville: Liturgical Press, 1996), 769.

it may have been a response to Pope John XXIII's initial prayer: "Renew your wonders in this our day as by a new Pentecost."[6]

In response to this new vision of the Church was the emergence of the Catholic Charismatic Renewal. This began on February 28, 1967 with some college students on a retreat at Duquesne University. They had been praying that the Holy Spirit would come to life within them in a totally new way. The result was that many of them received "the baptism in the Holy Spirit."

The baptism in the Holy Spirit is God responding to our prayer to

> So, what is the baptism in the Holy Spirit?

bring to life the power of the Holy Spirit that he has already given us. The baptism in the Holy Spirit (also called the release of the Holy Spirit,) is an experience of a deepened awareness of God's presence and love, an openness to the charismatic gifts of the Holy Spirit,[7] a

---

6   Quote is from *Humanae Salutis,* the opening speech of the Second Vatican Council, December 25, 1961, #23.

7   Included are the gifts of preaching, teaching, faith, healing, miracles, prophecy, the discernment of spirits, the gift of tongues and the interpretation of tongues. (See Romans 12: 6–8 and 1 Corinthians 12: 4–10 as examples.)

love of the scriptures, a love of the sacraments, an awareness of spiritual warfare, a desire to evangelize, and a love for the Church.[8]

Stemming from a multidenominational charismatic move of the Holy Spirit beginning in the 1950s and '60s [9] the Catholic Charismatic Renewal was a response to the new vision of the Church wrought by the Second Vatican Council. If the people were to take on a more active role in the Catholic Church, it was only by the power of the Holy Spirit that they would be able to do so.

In an address given to leaders of the Charismatic Renewal on July 15, 2015, Pope Francis quoted Cardinal Joseph Suenens saying: "The first error that must be avoided is including the Charismatic Renewal in the category of a Movement. It is not a specific Movement; the Renewal is . . . a current of grace, a renewing breath of the Spirit for all members of the

---

8   Patti Gallagher-Mansfield has a more detailed list of the effects of the baptism in the Holy Spirit in her book, *As by a New Pentecost,* p. 61.

9   Fr. Dennis Bennett, an Episcopalian priest, introduced the experience of the baptism in the Holy Spirit to his congregation in Van Nuys, California. Although ousted by his congregation, his continued preaching and writing began a charismatic move in several mainstream denominations. See *Nine-O clock in the Morning,* by Dennis Bennett.

Church, laity, religious, priests, and bishops. It is a challenge for us all."

Pope Francis also quot-ed the Cardinal as saying, "May the Charismatic Renewal disappear as such and be transformed into a

> The Charismatic Renewal is a current of grace, a renewing breath of the Spirit.

Pentecostal grace for the whole Church: to be faithful to its origin, the river must lose itself in the ocean."[10] In oth-er words, the experience of the baptism in the Holy Spirit should not be identified with the Charismatic Renewal per se, but with the whole Church.[11] These statements by Cardinal Suenens were made in 1975.

Many years later, this is still the view of the leader-ship in the Catholic Charismatic Renewal. Everyone who has been baptized, and especially those who have been confirmed, should be experiencing a deepened (deepening) love for God, an awareness of the gifts of the Holy Spirit, and a desire to share their faith with others. This should be the normal Catholic/Christian experience.

---

10 Pope Francis, address given to leaders of the Charismatic Renewal on July 15, 2015.

11 Pope Francis is paraphrasing Cardinal Suenens. The exact quote can be found in Cardinal Suenens's book, *A New Pentecost?* pp. 111 and 113.

On one level, this immersion of the baptism of the Holy Spirit into the normal Catholic life has already taken place. Many who had formerly been active in attending charismatic prayer meetings are now more involved with ministering in their own parishes. They received a spiritual awakening through the baptism in the Holy Spirit and have been called to serve outside of the charismatic prayer group.

And, as many have discovered, the charismatic prayer meeting is not the only place people are experiencing the baptism in the Holy Spirit. As we're told in John 3:8 "The wind (or the spirit) blows where it wills." An example of this is the ACTS retreat that was born in San Antonio, Texas in 1987.

Based on the Cursillo retreat, ACTS (an acronym for Adoration, Community, Theology, and Service) has enabled many of its participants to experience an intimate awareness of God's love for them and his presence in their lives. Listening to some of the men and women who have made an ACTS retreat and seeing the fruit of their experience sounds a lot like the baptism in the Holy Spirit.

One retreatant, Art Garcia, wrote:

My initiation to ACTS made me feel the joy of fellowship, worshiping God as a group, emulating the Apostles. As I later served on team, facilitating the retreat, I saw the transformation of the retreatants as they came closer to the Lord. Some of them broken, alone, or searching, transformed themselves into men of faith with a life-long commitment to God. Through ACTS I have seen many lives change in a miraculous way.

Another retreatant from ACTS, Andrew Ortiz, wrote:

I had been asked [to attend an ACTS retreat] for about four years. I refused. One day my friend asked me to attend, and I said maybe. He took it as a yes and registered me and even came to pick me up. In attending the retreat, I learned more about God, the Holy Spirit, and our Catholic faith. The Holy Spirit shook me to the core. I have now been clean from drugs for five and a half years. My Catholic faith is now very strong.

Still another retreatant, Ethel Garcia, had the following experience:

> Before attending an ACTS Retreat, I was trying to get closer to God, but I felt like I wasn't quite getting there. I know it is a lifetime process, but I guess I felt I wasn't worthy enough. During the ACTS Retreat I really felt God reaching out to me and telling me he really loved me. I came out of the retreat finally feeling I was on the path God wanted me to be on. I not only felt closer to Him, but I also felt closer to my friends and family members. I feel more connection, love, and compassion for all human beings. I have a long way to go in my journey to Jesus, but I feel that through what I experienced in ACTS I am on the right road and with the help of the Holy Spirit I will continue down that road.

These are examples from people I know, but it shows that the power of the Holy Spirit has transformed their lives as it had those in the Charismatic Renewal. In the same way, those in Cursillo, Antioch weekend, Search, and even a Life Teen weekend will attest to having had a similar experience.

The truth is that "Baptism in the Holy Spirit" is captive to no camp, whether liberal or conservative.

Nor is it identified with any one movement, nor with one style of prayer, worship, or community. On the contrary . . . baptism in the Holy Spirit belongs to the Christian inheritance of all those sacramentally initiated into the church."[12]

In addressing the International Conference on the Charismatic Renewal in the Catholic Church on May 19, 1975 Pope Paul V1 said: "How then could this 'spiritual renewal' not be an 'opportunity' for the Church and for the world."[13] Cardinal Yves Congar, one of the chief architects of Vatican II, has called the Renewal, "a grace that God has given to the times that we are living in."[14]

In 1992 Saint Pope John Paul II said, "The emergence of the Renewal following the Second Vatican Council was a particular gift of the Holy Spirit to the Church."[15] It is my opinion that what these

---

12 Kilian McDonnell and George T. Montague, *Christian Initiation and Baptism in the Holy Spirit* (Collegeville: The Liturgical Press, 1994), 382.

13 Pope Paul VI, "To Participants of the 3rd International Convention of the Catholic Charismatic Renewal," (May 19, 1975), Vatican website.

14 Yves Congar, *I Believe in the Holy Spirit, Book 2* (New York: Herder Crossroad, 2005), 158.

15 Pope John Paul II, "Address of His Holiness John Paul II to the Council of the 'International Catholic Charismatic Renewal Office,'" (March 14, 1992), Vatican website.

Church leaders are talking about is not the Catholic Charismatic Renewal itself, but the baptism in the Holy Spirit.

In an address Pope Francis gave to leaders of the Catholic Charismatic Renewal on June 8, 2019, he said:

> You asked me to tell you what the Pope and the Church expect from . . . the entire Charismatic Renewal . . . I expect this movement . . . to share baptism in the Holy Spirit with everyone in the Church. It is the grace you have received. Share it! Don't keep it to yourselves![16]

Even though the term "Baptism in the Holy Spirit" is associated with the Catholic Charismatic Renewal, it refers to an experience that is common to many different groups in the Catholic Church. The reason this experience is often born within these groups is because they provide a framework for promoting this grace.

Groups like Cursillo and Acts do this through their retreats and seminars. In the Catholic Charismatic Renewal, it is done through a series of talks called the

---

16 Pope Francis, "Address of His Holiness Pope Francis to Participants in the International Conference of Leaders of the Catholic Charismatic Renewal International Service-Charis," (June 8, 2019), Vatican website.

Life in the Spirit Seminar. The Steubenville retreat weekend has been very successful in bringing this renewal to youth. There is a group called Alpha that is bringing people into a personal relationship with Jesus Christ through videos, discussion, and fellowship.

I'm sure there are other groups that can make the same claim. Those who have had these spiritual experiences are hungering and thirsting to know God more, and there is more that God wants to give them through the gifts of the Holy Spirit!

There are several gifts of the Holy Spirit that are mentioned in sacred scripture. Some of these are mentioned in Isaiah 11:2–3, Romans 12:6–8, 1 Corinthians 12: 4–10 and Ephesians 4:11–12. These are not all the gifts of the Holy Spirit. There are other gifts that can be found in scripture, and God can invent a gift of the Holy Spirit at will. These are presented, though, to give people an understanding of what some of the gifts are, to discern the gifts they might have, and to discover opportunities for their use.

Someone might ask why this experience of the baptism in the Holy Spirit and the charismatic gifts are not encouraged from the pulpit? The truth is they *are* taught from the pulpit. Whenever the priest or deacon delivers a homily about God's love, growing in a deeper relationship with God, and serving, they are inadvertently talking about the baptism in the Holy Spirit.

There is the assumption the Holy Spirit is going to empower the congregation to follow through on the message given. When we receive the sacraments, it is presumed that the power of the Holy Spirit is going to awaken within us the grace to serve.

It is for no reason that RCIA participants are taught that they are going to receive the power and the gifts of the Holy Spirit when they are confirmed. There is the belief that something real is going to happen. Children from elementary grades up through high school are taught about the power of the Holy Spirit. It is expected to be the normal Catholic experience. The instruction is correct. What are often not taught, though, are the charismatic gifts of the Holy Spirit, and how those gifts can be used in everyday life.

One final point is that the sacraments set a foundation for the experience of the baptism in the Holy Spirit. It is through the grace of the sacraments that a hunger and a thirst for more of God is created, causing a sensitivity to the Holy Spirit to work in us. But we need to receive the sacraments with the right disposition.[17] We have to want the power of God's grace when we receive the sacraments.

Receiving the sacraments in this way will create a hunger and a thirst to know God more. It is this unquenchable hunger for God that will draw someone to seek the power of the Holy Spirit. It is in this spiritual quest that we will discover the gifts God has given us.

---

17 See the *Constitution on the Sacred Liturgy,* #11.

CHAPTER 3

The What, How, and Why of the Gifts of the Holy Spirit

What Are the Gifts of the Holy Spirit?

A story in the book of Acts tells about St. Paul asking a group of Christians if they received the Holy Spirit when they became believers (Acts 19:1–7). They responded that they didn't even know that there was any such thing as the Holy Spirit to be received. By inquiring further Paul discovered the believers had only been baptized in the name of John. When he baptized them in the name of Jesus they were filled with the Holy Spirit and began to speak in tongues and to prophesy.

In Confirmation and RCIA classes students are taught that the seven gifts of the Holy Spirit are wisdom, understanding, counsel, fortitude, knowledge, piety, and fear of the Lord. These are dispositions of the heart enabling the newly confirmed to be guided by the Holy Spirit. They are sometimes called "holiness gifts" because their purpose is to make us sensitive to the guidance of the Holy Spirit, which will make us holy. That's what happens when someone is guided by the power of the Holy Spirit.

The Church gets these gifts from Isaiah 11:2–3 where the prophet is describing the anointing that will be given to the Messiah:

> The spirit of the Lord shall rest
> upon him: a spirit of wisdom and
> of understanding,
> a spirit of counsel and of
> strength,
> a spirit of knowledge and of fear
> of the Lord,
> and his delight shall be the
> fear of the Lord. (NAB)

These are gifts that everyone receives with the sacraments of baptism and confirmation. As we are commissioned to be Jesus's disciples in the world, it is logically presumed that we will receive the same gifts he did. It makes sense. Their purpose is to develop within us an attitude of docility to the Holy Spirit, enabling the Holy Spirit to guide us toward a life of holiness. They are a part of what makes us the new creation that a life in Christ should.[18]

But there is no place in scripture that refers to these dispositions as being the only gifts of the Holy Spirit. And when St. Paul does talk about the gifts of the Holy Spirit in his letters, he doesn't mention them at all. The reason for this is because Paul was specifically referring to the service gifts he saw present in the church of his day.

The gifts of service that St. Paul mentions in Romans 12:6–8 are: prophecy, serving, teaching, encouragement, giving, leadership, and mercy. In 1 Corinthians 12:8–10 St. Paul adds the gifts of wisdom, knowledge, faith, healing, miracles, the discernment of spirits, tongues, and the interpretation of tongues. And in Ephesians 4:11 he lists the gifts of apostles, evangelists, and pastors. These are not the only gifts of the Holy Spirit but are the ones that St. Paul saw functioning in the early church.

It is important for us, though, not to look at some of the gifts of the Holy Spirit as being more important

---

18 "Whoever is in Christ is a new creation: the old things have passed away; behold, new things have come" (1 Corinthians 5:17).

than others. St. Paul addressed this in his analogy of the body in Romans 12:3–8, and 1 Corinthians 12:14–26. In summary, he said that all the parts in the body have a different function, but they need each other for the body to function properly.

In the same way, all the gifts in the body of Christ are equally important. Furthermore, it is

> If there isn't love then all the gifts are meaningless.

those gifts we do not give much attention to that are the most important. And to top it off if there isn't love then all the gifts are meaningless. It must be remembered, though, that there are gifts of the Holy Spirit St. Paul doesn't even mention, gifts such as: leading people in worship through music, having a sense of liturgy, ministering through the media, and so on.

And then, of course, God can invent a gift of the Holy Spirit whenever and however he wants to. What is important is to be aware of what some of these gifts are, and how God might be calling us to use them.

Jesus had a purpose for telling the apostles, and us through the Gospel,

Amen, amen, I say to you, whoever believes in me will do the works that I do, and will do greater ones than these, because I am going to the Father (John 14:12, NAB).

Jesus has given us gifts of the Holy Spirit to be his hands and his feet in the world today. They enable us to do the things that Jesus did and even more.

If we don't have any idea of what these gifts are, though, we're going to miss several opportunities to serve God through them. In this seminar we are going to focus on some of the gifts St. Paul mentions in scripture.

Gifts and Talents

It is important to remember that there is a difference between a gift of the Holy Spirit and a natural gift or talent. Someone may, for instance, be an extraordinarily good basketball player. There is a certain genetic ability they have for athletics, and they probably spent several hours fine-tuning their skill. They can still give thanks to God for their natural ability because "every perfect gift is from above" (James 1:17, NAB). However, the basketball player will still have their athletic ability whether they have the Holy Spirit or not.

The reason we receive baptism/confirmation and the gifts of the Holy Spirit is so we can continue to minister in Jesus's name. Having a natural ability for playing sports, academics, entertainment, or any other skill by itself is not going to win souls for Jesus Christ. The purpose of the gifts of the Holy Spirit is so we can win others for Jesus.

Now, it is true that a gift of the Holy Spirit can be added to a natural ability. Someone with a natural gift of teaching, for instance, can also receive an anointed gift of teaching. Once someone has surrendered a natural ability to Jesus, the Lord will often anoint that skill, enabling it to be used for his purpose. But it can also happen that someone without a natural gift for teaching can become an anointed teacher through the gift of the Holy Spirit.

Another example: a parishioner learns there is a need for teachers in the catechetical program at her parish. She never thought about teaching before or ever taught a class. Suddenly, though, there is a quickening in her heart. She contacts the religious education director, and before she knows it, she's teaching a class. It might be difficult for her in the beginning, but eventually she begins to catch on. She perseveres and suddenly a gift for teaching begins to emerge.

Spiritual gifts, just like natural gifts, grow with their use. We often begin to use natural gifts because there is a certain facility we have for them. Spiritual gifts begin to emerge principally because we are drawn to serving in a certain way. Although we may not have a natural skill for serving in a particular way, there is a hunger in the heart that motivates us to act. This can happen with leadership, administration, serving, or with any of the gifts of the Holy Spirit.

Sometimes these gifts are obvious and at other times they are harder to see. A parishioner told me it occurred to him one day he had a gift for leadership because he often found himself in leadership positions. He never thought about this skill as being a gift of the Holy Spirit, but it suddenly became obvious to him that it was.

Sometimes our gifts will be pointed out to us by someone else. Several years ago, a friend of mine told me I have a gift of having mercy. As I'll share later, that was not what I wanted to hear at the time, but mercy is a gift of the Holy Spirit.

My pastor and others claim that I have a gift for preaching. I've seen myself preach on TV, and I'm not convinced, but I'll take their word for it. They're encouraging a gift they see in me. We can also ask God for a gift we would like to have. There is no guarantee he will give us that gift, but we can rest assured God will give us the gift or gifts we need.

The Gifts in Church History

It is interesting to see how the use of some of the gifts of the Holy Spirit have evolved throughout Church history. The story begins in the book of Acts with Jesus's followers having a life-changing encounter with the Holy Spirit.

They were hiding from the Jewish authorities in fear of being tortured for their association with Jesus. They were also seeking a sign from God to let them know what they were supposed to do. Jesus had been their guide for the last three years and they had hoped he was going to become the king of Israel. Even before his ascension into heaven the apostles asked, "Lord, are you at this time going to restore the kingdom to Israel?" (Acts 1:6, NAB)

When the day of Pentecost came, they were praying in an upper room. Suddenly, there was the sound of a strong wind, and tongues of fire appeared on each one of them. They were all filled with the Holy Spirit and began to worship God in languages none of them knew. We'll talk more about these languages in the chapter on the word gifts. It can safely be said, though, that they were overwhelmed with joy as they boldly proclaimed God's praises.

There are some who believe it was only the apostles who were present in the upper room on the day of Pentecost. Scripture does tell us, though, that at least 120 of Jesus's followers were gathered for the selection of Matthias to replace Judas Iscariot. It is logical to assume this same group was praying together on the day of Pentecost.

So, when they all made their united, joyful sound, many of the Jewish people were drawn to it. They wondered what all the raucous was about! Remember, Pentecost was one of three feasts where every Jewish man was required to offer a sacrifice in Jerusalem if it was at all possible for him to do so. Consequently, there would have been a multitude of people listening to this sound.

At this point, Peter opened-up to his gift of teaching and preaching. This man who had three times denied that he even knew Jesus stood up before the Jewish multitude and preached a sermon so powerful that three thousand souls were added that day (Acts 2:41). That number soon grew to five thousand men (Acts 4:4), to say nothing of women and children. The reason for this growth was undoubtably due to the change people saw in the believer's lives, and the wonderous works done at the apostle's hands. (See Acts 2:43 as an example of the community that had formed.)

The Gifts Since the Early Days

Even though the book of Acts speaks of the unity that existed in the early church, we know this wasn't always the case. Each community had their own share of problems. In addressing these problems one of the topics Paul brought up in his letters were the gifts of the Holy Spirit.

Although we can assume St. Paul saw these gifts active in the church of his day, we don't often see the gifts of prophecy, tongues, the interpretation of tongues, healing, or miracles in our own time. It's taught by some, in fact, that many of these gifts were meant to establish the early church and are no longer needed. The question is when, why, and how did these gifts stop functioning in the church—or did they?

In the Didache, which is a church document dating from the first to the early second century CE, there is a description of how a community can recognize a true prophet.[19] During the first century, Justin Martyr (100–165 CE) believed the charismatic gifts were still active in the Church and would be until the end of time.[20] St. Irenaeus (120–200 CE) believed that not only did the charismatic gifts exist during his time, but that one could never count all the gifts of the Holy Spirit. [21]

Tertullian (155–240 CE) believed newly baptized adults received the charismatic gifts by asking for them.[25] Eusebius (260–339 CE) wrote in his commentary on the Psalms that the church still possessed the charismatic gifts, including "the word of wisdom, the word of knowledge, faith, healings, and tongues."[22]

St. Hillary of Poitiers (315–367 CE) believed the charismatic gifts of the Holy Spirit were still active in his day, as he mentions them several times in his work, *On the Trinity*.[23] He also taught that when a person is baptized, the Lord has pity on them in their weakness

---

19 The Didache, 11.7–11.12.
20 Yves Congar, *I Believe in the Holy Spirit, Book 1* (New York: Herder Crossroad, 2005), 65.
21 McDonnell and Montague, *Christian Initiation and Baptism in the Holy Spirit*, Second Revised Edition, Collegeville, MN. The Liturgical Press. 1994. 357.
22 McDonnell and Montague, *Christian Initiation and Baptism in the Holy Spirit*, 164.
23 Ibid. 176–179.

and feeds them spiritually with the seven gifts of the Holy Spirit: wisdom, understanding, counsel, strength, knowledge, piety, and fear of the Lord.[28] St. Hillary saw both the Isaiah and charismatic gifts as being a part of the Christian experience.

By the end of the fourth century, though, the charismatic gifts seem to have decreased in the Church. There were still gifts of teaching, leadership, ministry, and dispositions of holiness. Miracles were still taking place,[24] but the charismatic gifts mentioned by St. Paul were rarely seen. One of the reasons for their decline may have been because the laity had no idea these gifts were in existence.[25]

As the charisms decreased among the laity so did the enthusiasm that was seen in the early church. In longing for the days when the charisms played a more dominant role St. John Chrysostom (c. 347–407) wrote, "The present church is like a woman who has fallen from her former prosperous days."[26]

---

24 St. Augustine, *City of God, Book 2,* (New York: Doubleday, 1958), chapters 8–9. In the fifth century St. Augustine wrote about several miracles that he knew about.
25 McDonnell and Montague, *Christian Initiation and Baptism in the Holy Spirit,* 114.
26 Ibid. 288.

In the fifth century, St. Augustine, (354–430) listed the gifts of Isaiah 11:2–3 as being the gifts of the Holy Spirit. Their purpose, as far as the laity were concerned, were more to help one grow in holiness and faith than to serve. This teaching may have been due to the church's emphasis on clergy and liturgy over the laity.

In any case, this continued to be the thinking of the church to the twentieth century. There was one charismatic gift, however, that continued to flourish throughout the Middle Ages (fifth to fifteenth century CE). It was called "jubilation." This will be covered more in the chapter on the word gifts.

Questions for Thought and Discussion

The What, How, and Why of the Gifts of the Holy Spirit

1. Do you have any questions about the teaching?

2. What is the specific purpose of the gifts of the Holy Spirit in Isaiah 11:2–3?

3. What is the purpose of the gifts of the Holy Spirit that St. Paul mentions in his letters?

4. What are some possible gifts of the Holy Spirit not mentioned by St. Paul?

5. In John 14:12 Jesus tells us that we will do even greater works than his. What do you think he meant by this? What does this mean for you?

6. Have you ever experienced the power of the Holy Spirit flowing through you? Briefly describe this experience. How did this experience affect you?

CHAPTER 4

Daily Experiencing the Seven Gifts: Wisdom, Understanding, Counsel, Fortitude, Knowledge, Piety, and Fear of the Lord

The Catholic Church teaches that the seven gifts of the Holy Spirit are given to everyone at baptism. These are strengthened at confirmation, and the recipient can grow in the charismatic gifts as well.

But the reason everyone receives the seven gifts of the Holy Spirit is because they increase our sensitivity to the guidance of the Holy Spirit. This will ultimately make us holy, and holiness is the goal of every follower of Jesus Christ. As Saint Pope John Paul 11 wrote in his apostolic letter, *Novo Millenio Ineuente:* "To ask catechumens: 'Do you wish to receive Baptism?' means at the same time to ask them: 'Do you wish to become holy?' " (#31)

The seven gifts of the Holy Spirit (sometimes called the holiness gifts), may not appear to be as exciting as some of the more miraculous charisms. They are not filled with the power, enthusiasm, and self-importance that miracles, healing, and prophecy might bring. Nonetheless, holiness is what our church and world need more today than any other gift of the Holy Spirit. We need the gifts of holiness to stamp out the world-view of secularism that is dominating our culture.

Secularism is the belief that faith and religion have

> **What is secularism?**

little if any value at all. We can see this in the media, politics, and the values that are shaping our culture today.

In light of Isaiah 5:20,[27] secularism calls evil good and good evil. We can see this with the acceptance of abortion, premarital sex, and the abhorrence of traditional Christian values. If anyone wants to "be cool" or culturally "with it," they're going to embrace the secular worldview.

In addition to its influence on our culture, the secular mentality has also infiltrated the Church in

---

27 Isaiah 5:50: "Ah! Those who call evil good, and good evil, who change darkness to light, and light into darkness, who change bitter to sweet and sweet into bitter!" (NAB)

the form of individualism. This worldview says that if we do not agree with the teachings of the Pope on doctrine or moral theology then he's probably wrong. It's this same attitude that caused Adam and Eve to eat the forbidden fruit. It's rebellion against authority and, ultimately, against God.

The only way our culture is going to be drawn away from secularism is by giving people something better: Jesus Christ. And the only way our culture is going to be drawn to Jesus is if they see Jesus in us—that is, by our becoming holy. That is why we've been given the Isaiah 11:2–3 gifts of the Holy Spirit. So, let's see what these holiness gifts of the Holy Spirit are.

The first is the gift of wisdom. Proverbs 9:10 tells us that "The beginning of wisdom is fear of the Lord" (NAB). The root of wisdom is loving God above all things. This is mentioned in scripture as being the first and greatest commandment (Deuteronomy 6:4–7, Matthew 22:37, Mark 12:30). If we put God first in our lives then we will want what he wants for us, and what God wants for us will always be for our good. It doesn't take a brilliant mind to understand that this is the beginning of wisdom.

Through wisdom God can help us put some priority in our lives. Is it more important for me to be on

> Wisdom helps us see things from God's perspective.

a multitude of church committees or to spend more time at home with my family? Is making more money really worth the cost? Is getting my own way really that important?

Wisdom is being able to look at the facts and discern the correct action to take. Not only is this gift helpful with making life decisions, it's also helpful in solving problems that can come up working in a committee. Wisdom asks the question, "Where is God in this, and what would he have me, or us, do?

Another way wisdom can help is with making moral decisions. Living in a world that is surrounded with multiple voices vying for our allegiance, wisdom helps us to discern the best voice to listen to. Since we have been created by God and for God, the voice we want to listen to is the one that is going to give greater glory to God. It helps us listen to those voices that are giving greater glory to God and to filter out those that are not.

Wisdom gives us the ability to freely make that choice. This is important because the Church doesn't want us to adhere to a certain moral code simply because they tell us it's the right thing to do. They want us to follow Church teaching because we know it to be the right thing to do.[28] This is what comes with the gift of Wisdom.

The second gift is understanding. This gift gives us an insight into what God is doing with us. We may be going through a series of

> The gift of understanding can help us know who we are in God's eyes.

trials like Job, but we have the awareness that God knows what he's doing. We can also see God's hand in spiritual dryness. For a while God's presence may have seemed to have always been with us when suddenly he's nowhere to be found.

The gift of understanding lets us know that in times of dryness and trials God can be closer than ever before. And we can even rejoice in our trials because we know that God is going to use them for our good (Romans 5:8, James 1:2-4.) The gift of understanding gives us the ability to have faith in what God is doing with us even though we may not have a clear picture of it.

---

28 Pope Paul VI, *Gaudium et Spes,* #17 (December 7, 1985), Vatican website.

This can be helpful in assisting others through their spiritual journeys too. Although there is more involved with spiritual direction than knowing the ways of God, we can at least use this skill to remind people that God will never leave them. He is constantly working with them for their good. The gift of understanding can help us to comprehend the teachings of our faith. Some of the greatest teachers in the church would have been working from this gift.

And yet, one need not be a great intellect for the gift of understanding to be actively working within them. Having a basic understanding that one is infinitely loved by God is a tremendous benefit of this gift. There are many people in the world who do not have this understanding of God. They wonder why God allows suffering and evil to exist especially if he is a God of love.

More specifically they wonder why God has allowed evil and suffering to enter their own lives. Someone with the gift of understanding might not be able to articulate a specific reason for the existence of evil and suffering, but they understand that God is present even in these times.

The third gift is counsel. Through this gift we know, almost by instinct, the correct way to act in a given situation. We know it because we are being guided by the Holy Spirit. Through

> Through the gift of counsel we know, almost by instinct, the correct way to act in a given situation.

this gift we have practiced listening to the Holy Spirit and doing what the Holy Spirit says.

The question is, how do we know when it is the Holy Spirit speaking to us? This is a good question.

We learn how to listen to the Holy Spirit by listening to him. When we pray, we often spend more time listening to ourselves than to God. If we want to get in touch with listening to the Holy Spirit, we need to spend time listening to God in silence. In psalm 46:10 or 11 (depending on the translation) we are told, "Be still and know that I am God!" (NAB)[29]

When we ask the Holy Spirit to speak to us, he will. We may sense his words coming to us from the depths of our hearts or we may not. If nothing else,

---

29 We definitely need to spend time silently listening to God in prayer. But CCC 2639 reminds us that "praise" is also important for listening to the Holy Spirit.

we are taking the time to listen. We can also practice listening to the Holy Spirit with Lectio Divina. This is a technique of reading a verse of scripture and listening to God speak to us through it.[30]

Another way to practice listening to the Holy Spirit is to use the four cardinal virtues in daily life.[31] These are prudence, justice, fortitude, and temperance. **Prudence** is simply looking before you leap. It is weighing the pros and cons in a given situation and making the most reasonable choice. It is taking the time to think about and pray about an act before making a decision.

The virtue of **Justice** lives out the two greatest commandments: love God first and love your neighbor as yourself. The irony in this virtue is that one cannot love God without loving one's neighbor.[32] Therefore, if we keep from others something that rightly belongs to them, we're keeping this from God as well. We are

---

30 Basically, there are four parts to Lectio Divina. 1: Read and reflect on what was read. 2: Read and imagine yourself in the scene. 3: Read and have a conversation with God. 4: Read and ask God what he expects of us. It's a little bit more detailed than this but it all involves listening.

31 The Cardinal virtues are described in greater detail in CCC 1806, 1807, 1808, and 1809.

32 "If anyone says, 'I love God,' but hates his brother, he is a liar." (1 John 4:20)

stealing it from him because, ultimately, everything belongs to God.

The Catechism of the Catholic Church tells us: "In his use of things man should regard the external goods he legitimately owns not merely as exclusive to himself but common to others also" (CCC 2404.) This is in the section dealing with the seventh commandment: "You shall not steal."[33] We need to be providing the basic living needs for those who have not because it is rightfully theirs anyway (CCC 2446.) Practicing the virtue of justice invites us to prayerfully reflect on our obedience to follow Jesus's command to love our neighbor.

Fortitude or courage gives us the grace to say "No" to temptations to sin, "Yes" to sharing your faith with others, and "Yes" to living by our moral values. St. James gave a good maxim for this when he wrote, "Be doers of the word and not hearers only, deluding yourselves" (James 1:22, NAB). Fortitude says that we not only talk the talk, but that we walk the walk. It is having the courage to be an authentic disciple of Jesus Christ. The virtue of courage, which is also a gift, calls us to seek God's strength whenever we're afraid.

---

33 The section on the seventh commandment is in CCC 2401–2449.

Temperance is the virtue that strives to live in moderation. We are naturally drawn to that which gives us the greatest pleasure and satisfaction. This quest for satisfaction can be a good thing when it motivates us to improve ourselves and others. However, the desire for pleasure by itself can cause us to use and abuse ourselves, others and the material goods God has given us. The virtue of temperance gives us a respect for, and a proper use of God's creation. The virtue of moderation enables us to seek God's guidance regarding the use of his gifts.

When we seek to live by each of these virtues, it gives us the time needed to listen to the Holy Spirit. This is how we grow in the gift of counsel. As we discipline ourselves to listen to the Holy Spirit the gift of counsel will come to life within us.

We already talked about the fourth holiness gift of fortitude when discussing the virtues, so we'll go right into the fifth holiness gift, which is **knowledge.**

> Knowledge is the ability to understand truths about God.

Having an intimate knowledge of the existence of God, His infinite love, and the existence of the Trinity all come from the gift of knowledge.

A typical Catholic might not be able to eloquently argue truths about God, but she knows them to be true anyway. People are able to serve others with this gift by giving them hope. Their faith and trust in a God whom they *know* can be very contagious.

The sixth gift is piety. This gift enables us to be respectful of God and our Church. It is a sense that our

> Piety shows respect for God and the Church.

lives are based on our relationship with God. Having a profound respect for God and the Church tells others that there must really be something important going on.

When someone speaks in a respectful manner about their faith others are drawn to listen. They might even think, "What does this person know that I don't?" When someone visiting a church spots a parishioner actively involved with the liturgy and respectfully praying the Mass, they're going to be drawn to that.

One day my wife was able to plant some seeds in the heart of a little boy attending Mass with his mom. The little boy pointed to my wife and said, "Mom, that lady looks like she likes going to Mass." And then he said, "I don't like going to Mass." I'm sure he would have rather been watching television or playing video games. Nonetheless, he will remember seeing someone who really looked like they enjoyed coming to Mass and it will get him to thinking. The gift of piety enables the recipient of this gift to evangelize in this manner.

The seventh gift is the fear of the Lord. This gift is the awareness that we do truly have an awesome God! Everything in the universe was created by God for us! All the laws of physics, the billions of galaxies, and the position of our planet in the solar system have been perfectly designed by God for us. And this God who created the entire universe, and has no beginning or end, loves each one of us personally. He is constantly present to us, thinking about us, and planning wonderous things for our lives.

In the commentary to his poem, "The Living Flame of Love," St. John of the Cross reminds us "that if a person is seeking God, his Beloved is seeking him much more."[34] We matter to God! We are important to him! How could we not want to shout

---

34 Kieran Kavanaugh OCD and Otilio Rodriguez OCD, trans., *The Collected Works of St. John of the Cross* (Washington, D.C.: Institute of Carmelite Studies, 1979), 620.

our praises out to God! This seventh gift enables us to know just how awesome God truly is! And because of this we have a fear of offending him. It's not so much a fear of being punished as a fear of offending such a wonderful, marvelous God. It is a call to obedience out of love.

The purpose of the seven gifts of the Holy Spirit in Isaiah 11:2–3 are to dispose us to the guidance and influence of the Holy Spirit, which will enable us to become holy. Everyone can benefit from using these gifts in their everyday life. Parents can benefit exceedingly from the seven Isaiah gifts in daily family life.

Youth can benefit in daily decision making, morality and discovering the path that God has for them. Employers, employees, politicians, and religious leaders can all benefit from these "holiness" gifts of the Holy Spirit. They are a part of the gift of the Holy Spirit that we received at baptism and confirmation.

What we need to do is start using them. It's like high performance fuel in the engine of an expensive racecar. Nothing's going to happen until we turn the key in the ignition. We need to start using the gifts God has given to us.

Questions for Thought and Discussion

Daily Experiencing the Seven Gifts:
Wisdom, Understanding, Counsel, Fortitude,
Knowledge, Piety, and Fear of the Lord

1. Do you have any questions concerning the holiness gifts of the Holy Spirit?

2. What is secularism and why is it a problem for the church today?

3. The gift of wisdom can be described as "seeing things from God's perspective." How can this gift help you to live a holy life?

4. The gift of understanding gives us an insight into what God is doing with us. How can this gift help you to live a holy life?

5. The gift of counsel helps us to know, almost by instinct, the correct way to act in a given situation. How can this gift help you to live a holy life?

6. The gift of fortitude is the strength to live a Christian life. Name a situation where this gift can help you to live a holy life.

7. The gift of knowledge gives us the ability to understand truths about God. Name a situation where this gift can help you to live a holy life.

8. The gift of piety helps us to be respectful of God and the church. Name a situation where this gift can help you to live a holy life.

9. The fear of the Lord is the gift that helps us to be in awe of Almighty God. How can this gift help you to live a holy life?

CHAPTER 5

Daily Experiencing the Word Gifts: Tongues, the Interpretation of Tongues, and Teaching

The gift of tongues is probably the most misunderstood gift of the Holy Spirit. Many Catholics are afraid or at least concerned about it because it hasn't been a part of their normal Catholic experience. And yet, Catholics in the Middle Ages would have had no problem with this gift at all.

The reason for this may be because it wasn't referred to as being the gift of tongues. The gift of tongues was seen as being a real language that enabled those with this gift to preach in foreign lands.[35] The gift of tongues that still existed as a form of praise was called "jubilation." St. Jerome (347–402 CE) wrote: "By the term 'jubilus' we understand that which neither in words nor syllables or letters nor speech is it

---

35 McDonnell and Montague, *Christian Initiation and Baptism in the Holy Spirit,* 366.

possible to express or comprehend how much man ought to praise God"[36]

In Romans 8:26 St. Paul mentions our inability to express ourselves in prayer. He writes that "the Spirit too comes to the aid of our weakness; for we do not know how to pray as we ought, but the Spirit himself intercedes with inexpressible groanings" (NAB). This sounds like what St. Jerome was referring to, and what today is called the gift of tongues.

St. John Chrysostom (347–407) wrote: "It is permitted to sing songs without words as long as the mind is focused on God."[37] In the sixth century Pope Gregory the Great (540–604) wrote: "By the term "jubilation" we mean a joy of the heart that cannot be expressed in speech, yet the person who is rejoicing makes this joy known in certain ways—this joy cannot be concealed, yet cannot be fully expressed (in words)."[38]

Pope Gregory also wrote: "Let angels therefore praise because they know such brightness; but let men

---

36 Quoted in *Sounds of Wonder: A Popular History of Speaking in Tongues in the Catholic Tradition,* by Eddie Ensley (New York/Ramsey: Paulist Press, 1977), 8.
37 Quoted in *Sounds of Wonder: Speaking in Tongues in the Catholic Tradition* by Eddie Ensley. 9
38 Ibid..17

who are limited by speech jubilate."[39] St. Augustine (354–430) wrote:

> What is jubilation? Joy that cannot be expressed in words. Yet the voice expresses what is conceived in the heart and cannot be expressed in words. This is jubilation. [40]

St. Teresa of Avila (1515–1582) also shared about jubilation. In her book *The Interior Castle,* she wrote:

> Our Lord sometimes gives the soul feelings of jubilation and a strange prayer it doesn't comprehend . . . What I'm saying seems like gibberish, but certainly the experience takes place in this way, for the joy is so excessive the soul wouldn't want to enjoy it alone but wants to tell everyone about it so that they might help this soul praise the Lord.[41]

There are several other examples that could be given to show the use of jubilation among the saints.

---

39 Ibid. 17.

40 Ibid, 8.

41 Kieran Kavanaugh OCD and Otilio Rodriguez OCD, trans., *The Collected Works of St. Teresa of Avila, Vol. 2.* (Washington, D.C.: Institute of Carmelite Studies, 1980), 395.

These few have been presented to show that the experience is not foreign to Catholic tradition. While it could be argued that the saints did not view jubilation as being the gift of tongues, their description of it sounds identical to what St. Paul was talking about in Romans 8:26. The primary purpose of the gift of tongues is for praise.

When we run out of words to praise God in our own language, there's the gift of tongues. And as we continue to praise God with the gift of tongues they will often become silent as we enter into a more quiet and contemplative adoration.

> When words are not enough to convey the level of praise that is intended, there is the gift of tongues.

Some people will say they used to pray in tongues but now they're drawn to contemplative prayer. There doesn't need to be the discrepancy at all. In fact, praying in tongues can lead into a quieter state of adoration and contemplation.

We can praise God in tongues whenever and wherever we want to. When we're in a situation where our praying in tongues might be offensive to someone, we can pray in tongues mentally. This is a great help when we're taking an exam or in a stressful situation. When I pray in tongues, even if it is done mentally, I can sense the power of the Holy Spirit praying through me.

The gift of tongues is a vocal expression of what the Holy Spirit is doing in the heart of the believer. But it is a language that is unknown to the person speaking it. There have been cases where the words spoken were understood as a specific language, but this will usually not be the case. Because of this, it is often argued that the gift of tongues is nothing more than nonsensical gibberish.

This may be the case. But in 2009 the Linguistic Society of America determined there to being 6,909 known languages.[42] This is to say nothing of languages that were once in use but have since died out. And then, of course, God can invent a language at a moment's notice. So, just because the meaning of the sounds being emitted is not understood by the people listening does not mean that someone's gift of tongues isn't a real language.

But even if the gift of tongues is nonsensical gibberish "The Lord looks into the heart" (1 Samuel 16:7). The Lord knows what's in someone's heart, whether

---

42 My source for this is https://www.linguisticsociety.org/content/how-many-languages-arethere-world.

it's gibberish, a forgotten language, or just one that is unknown to the listeners.

Another purpose for the gift of tongues is praying for others. If we're praying with someone for a healing, for instance, we may not really know what their need is. But the Holy Spirit does. If the person we're praying with is not familiar with this gift, and we're concerned about offending them, we can pray in tongues silently. When we're praying in tongues with someone, we're praying in faith that the Holy Spirit knows exactly what their need is.

It is true, of course, that we don't have to use tongues when we're praying for or with someone. The Holy Spirit knows what the need is, whether we pray in tongues or not. One advantage of praying in tongues, though, is that it enables us to minister more to the person we're praying with. We can pray, "Lord, meet their need. Thy will be done. Heal them from whatever is causing their pain," and then it's all over.

When we pray in tongues, though, we can minister to them longer because we don't have to worry about running out of words. This is good because praying in tongues with someone will often give them a sense of peace.

Another use of the gift of tongues is what St. Paul calls the interpretation of tongues. During a charismatic prayer meeting, or even during private prayer, a sense will be given to someone to pray in their tongue. If it is during a charismatic prayer meeting the recipient will then give the gist of the Holy Spirit's message in a known language. It is not a direct translation. How do we know if the message given is from the Lord? Every presumed message from God needs to be spiritually discerned.

Most messages are going to be like, "I love you my people; you are my people; I rejoice in your praises." A message like this is safe because God is probably speaking these words to us twenty-four hours a day anyway. But for messages that are not as clean-cut we have the gift of discernment of spirits (1 Corinthians 12:10).

This gift will send up a red flag or cause the leaders to feel uneasy when a message isn't from the Lord. It takes away the peace from those discerning the message and will affect others in the same way. (This discernment of spirits is mentioned more in chapter 7.)

When someone asks God to receive the gift of tongues it might come right away or not for some time. Why this happens God only knows. But it has absolutely nothing to do with the level of God's love for them or their personal holiness. God works with everyone in the way and in the time that is best for them.

Sometimes, though, God will grant someone the gift of tongues and they don't know how to open up to it. One remedy for this is to start talking gibberish, or baby talk. This at least gets the tongue to start moving. As the worshiper continues to praise God in their tongue, they will notice their speech becoming more articulate. As the sounds flow fluently from their lips they will sense the Holy Spirit praying through them.

Are there arguments against praying in tongues? Of course, there are. But it is one of the gifts of the Holy Spirit mentioned by St. Paul. It has been a part of the Catholic experience, and there are many Catholics today who pray in tongues. Furthermore, it is mentioned as a viable gift in the Catechism of the Catholic Church (CCC 2003). There's no reason for anyone to fear it, or to be concerned about its validity in the Catholic Church.

The Gift of Teaching

I like to call the gift of tongues and the interpretation of tongues "word gifts" because they minister through the spoken word. I like to also include with the word gifts the charism of "teaching." The teacher is someone who can express their faith in a way that gives encouragement and instruction to others. This gift can be used in speaking at conferences; giving retreats such as ACTS, Cursillo, Life in the Spirit Seminars, and LIGHT; teaching a catechism class, preaching, and so on. It can also be used in sharing our faith with others.

The purpose of this gift is to enable the listener to hear the Holy Spirit speaking to them. If all the listeners come away with is admiration for the teacher's skill, the teacher has not done their job.

> The purpose of the gift of teaching is to enable the listener to hear the Holy Spirit speaking to them through the teacher's words.

I am reminded of the old story where a trained actor recited the twenty-third psalm at a church fiesta. The people whistled, applauded, and cheered after his presentation.

But then an old man in the audience walked up to the podium, recited the twenty-third psalm, and sat down. There was a silent awe that came over the people when the old man finished. Some were brought to tears. The professional actor went up to the podium again and said, "The difference in our presentations is that I know the psalm; the old man knows the shepherd."

In the same way, we should not be drawn to the eloquence of the teacher, but to the simplicity of the Holy Spirit speaking to us. The purpose of the teacher is to clean out our spiritual ears, enabling us to clearly hear the Holy Spirit's voice. So, it is not necessary for a teacher to be a scholar, have an advanced degree in theology, or even a high I.Q. A teacher is someone who has an advanced love for God, and the desire to share their faith with others.

It is important to remember the gift of teaching comes from God, and a natural gift of teaching comes from the intellect. They are two different things. Someone can have both, of course, but the gift of teaching can also come to someone without the genetic predisposition for it. They may find it difficult to teach in the beginning, but as their focus becomes less on themselves and more on God, it will become easier for them.

What I am saying is if someone has a hunger to share their faith through teaching, they should do it. It is only in this way they will discover whether they have a gift for it or not. It usually takes a while to grow in any gift, and if the hunger for teaching is still there, they should keep doing it. The real test will come with the response they get from their listeners. The question that needs to be asked is, are the listeners being drawn more to God, or to the teacher's presentation?

One final point on teaching. In *Evangeli Nuntiandi #41,* Pope Paul V1 says "Modern man listens more willingly to witnesses than to teachers, and if he does listen to teachers, it is because they are witnesses." Even if one has the gift of teaching, their words are going to be more effective if they are coupled with firsthand experience.

Personal testimony and true stories are very affective for this.

Questions for Thought and Discussion

Daily Experiencing the Word Gifts: Tongues, the Interpretation of Tongues, and Teaching

1. Do you have any questions about the gift of tongues, or the interpretation of tongues?

2. Do you have any questions about the gift of teaching?

3. What are some ways the gift of tongues can be used in everyday life?

4. How could the interpretation of tongues be used in everyday life?

5. What problems might an intelligent person have with the gift of teaching?

6. What attributes should a good teacher have?

7. Why do you think praying in tongues is not necessarily a sign of holiness?

8. How could you use the interpretation of tongues outside of a charismatic prayer meeting?

CHAPTER 6

Daily Experiencing the Gifts of Power: Healing and Miracles

Healing and the working of miracles are both gifts of the Holy Spirit. The New American Bible calls miracles "mighty deeds" but it means the same thing. A miracle is an extraordinary event that cannot be explained by the laws of nature or science. It is the same way with a miraculous healing. There is no scientific reason why a healing should have taken place, but it did.

For instance, there are several examples of miraculous healings that have been documented taking place from the waters of Lourdes. One of the first Lourdes miracles took place with a two-year-old boy named Justin Bouhort in 1858. He had been extremely sick from birth, was unable to walk, and his prognosis was that he was not going to improve.

In a moment of desperation his mother lifted her son up and carried him to the spring at Massabielle. She prayed before the grotto and then lowered her son into the spring, keeping him there for some time. She then lifted him up and returned home. That night Justin slept peacefully, and in the morning, it was obvious his condition had improved.

Justin quickly recovered and soon began to walk. He lived a long life and was even able to attend St. Bernadette's canonization in 1923. The doctor who had been treating him, Dr. Dozous, documented that Justin's healing could only be attributed to a miraculous intervention.[43]

A similar situation took place with a friend of mine, Deacon Frank Smith. In 1996 he was diagnosed with bladder cancer. He received surgery to remove the cancer, but the cancer returned. This was to be his situation for the next nine years. The cancer was removed and would return again.

By 2005 the cancer was progressing rapidly, and he needed to have another surgery right away. Just prior

---

43 The information about Justin Bouhort was obtained from the website: http://www.miraclehunter.com/marian_apparitions/approved_apparitions/lourdes/miracles1.html.

to the surgery, though, Deacon Frank went to Lourdes to bathe in the miraculous waters. Shortly after returning from Lourdes he went to the hospital for the surgery he had previously been scheduled for. When he woke up from the anesthesia he was told they couldn't find any cancer at all.[44] The only explanation for his healing was that he was miraculously healed from the water at Lourdes. So, miraculous healings still do take place.

There are also times, though, when God works within natural law to bring about a healing. For instance, God expects us to go to the doctor when we get sick. After all, scripture tells us the doctor receives his wisdom for healing from God.[45] However, if it is God's will to heal someone in a supernatural (or miraculous) way, it is entirely up to him. We should never presume to know the mind of God.

Several years ago, my wife knew a lady who stopped taking the medicine the doctors had given her for stomach cancer. She did this to give proof of her faith in God. She eventually died. She might have died even if she had continued taking the medication,

---

44 This story was told to me by Deacon Frank Smith. He has given permission to tell his story here.

45 The book of Sirach 38:2 (this is also called the book of Ecclesiasticus).

but she should not have given up one of God's means of bringing about her healing. Using the wisdom God has given to doctors to heal us is not showing a lack of faith in God, it is how we show our faith in God.

There are, of course, miraculous healings that still do take place. When I was seven years old, I was in an automobile accident in Los Angeles, California. The doctors at the first hospital I was taken to said I was going to die and there was nothing that could be done for me. I was then taken to Children's Hospital in Hollywood. The prognosis there was pretty much the same, except they were going to do everything they could while I was still alive.

One day my mom asked the neurosurgeon what my prognosis was. He told her if I ever did regain consciousness I would be severely handicapped, requiring institutionalization for the rest of my life. She went into our parish church (St. Bruno's in Whittier) and surrendered my life to God. When she returned to the hospital, she was told that I had just regained consciousness following a nine-day coma. Three months later I was out of the hospital, walking and preparing to return to school.

When my mom thanked the neurosurgeon for all he had done he said, "Don't thank me, thank God."

Undoubtedly, the doctors' treatment and care added to my healing. But there was a certain point even the doctors knew was beyond their natural science.

A more recent example is when a friend prayed with me to receive a healing from the pain in my right knee. One day it started popping, leaving me with extreme pain in the joint. My orthopedist recommended that I stop doing leg exercises with weights and walking on the treadmill. This was to be a first level of treatment. After my friend prayed with me, though (three times over a three-week period), I am now free of pain and am as active in the gym as I was before.

My friend, Vince Montoya, does have a gift of healing and has seen many miraculous cures through his ministry. Not everyone has this gift, but God can work through anyone who asks to bring a healing to someone. There is no way we're going to know if we have this gift or if it's God's will to heal someone through us unless we're willing to pray with people.

When someone tells us about an ailment they're having, whether it be physical, psychological, or spiritual, we need to ask if we can pray for them. It's OK to remember their need in personal prayer, but we minister more to the whole person when we pray *with* them. One of the ways this can be done is by laying hands on someone's shoulder and praying with them.

In Luke 4:40 we're told this was how Jesus ministered to people when he prayed for their healing. This was also how the apostles prayed with people to receive the Holy Spirit (Acts 8:14–19,) and to anoint believers for a mission or a new position in the Church (Acts 6:5–6). So, if it was good enough for Jesus and the apostles it should be good enough for us. Some people don't like being touched, though, so it's always good to ask if we can lay our hands on them.

God can instantaneously work miracles from heaven, but his preferred method is often to work through us.[46] Scripture tells us how God used the pagan ruler, King Nebuchadnezzar, to purify the hearts of his people.[47] We're also told that God sent another pagan, Cyrus the Great, to set his people free from their Babylonian captivity. God can work through and with whomever he wills. So, why wouldn't God use a doctor or anyone of us to assist him in bringing healing to someone?

---

46 The purpose of the gifts of the Holy Spirit is for God to minister through us; see Romans 12:4–8 and 1 Corinthians 12:4–10.

47 Jeremiah 18:13–17, 21:1–14, 2 Chronicles 36:22–23.

I learned this when I prayed for my pastor for a healing from cancer. I sincerely believed that God was going to miraculously heal him. When I asked about his condition the next day, he said that he felt worse than the day before. I prayed with him once a week for three weeks with the same results. I began to think that maybe my prayers just weren't powerful enough to reach the ears of the Almighty. Afterward, he received medical treatment and today he is cancer free.

This is good news, but why didn't God answer my prayer? All I know is that God didn't answer my prayer in the way or the time that I wanted him to. However, my pastor didn't experience any of the pain or discomfort that is often associated with radiation therapy. Perhaps that was a part of God's answer to my prayer. It may be that his healing was more rapid or more complete than it otherwise would have been.

God only knows how he answered my prayer. But we are told in scripture that God does answer prayer.[48] Our job as believers is to expect that God will answer our prayer. It may not be in our preferred way or time,

---

48 See Matthew 18:19–20, 21:22, 7:7, Mark 11:24, Luke 11:9–13.

but that's as it should be because he is God and we are not. That's why 1 Thessalonians 5:18 encourages us to give thanks to God "In all circumstances . . . for this is the will of God for [us] in Christ Jesus."

But supernatural healing isn't the only way miracles can come to us. In the case of healing, God provides health where there once was suffering. Besides healing there are

> Miracles can be defined as God providing something that wasn't there before.

many areas where God has provided for the needs of his people. One rather famous incident took place with Fr. Rick Thomas, S.J., and his prayer group in El Paso, Texas.

On Christmas day in 1972 the prayer group brought food to feed the people who usually ate from the dump in Juarez, Mexico. They immediately could tell there was going to be a problem, though, because they had only brought enough food to feed 120 people, and 300 people showed up. What were they going to do once they ran out of food?

So, they kept serving and they kept trusting. They didn't know where the food was coming from, but there always seemed to be more food to serve. When they finished serving the 300 people, they still had enough food to donate to a local orphanage.[49] There are several other stories like this that can be found in the book, *Loaves and Fishes: Jesus and the Feeding of the Multitudes,* by Joseph D. Cieszinski. The stories in Joe's book show that God still does perform miracles.

One way we can receive a miracle in life is by asking God to provide one for us and believe that he's going to do it. Of course, God isn't going to perform some magic trick just to impress us. He doesn't need to do that. But if there is a need, we can pray for it and believe that God has heard and will answer our prayer. We need to believe, however, that the miracle will take place in God's way and time, not ours.

Sometimes God will answer our prayer by calling us to do our part. Several years ago my wife and I were doing volunteer work for a radio program called *Albuquerque Alive.* Our job was to record testimonies over the phone and edit them into brief segments for air play.

On one testimony a lady shared how God had met their financial need. They had been praying for a miracle when one day a little boy came to their door and gave them a bag with money in it. It was the exact

---

49 Joseph D. Cieszinski, *Loaves and Fishes: Jesus and the Feeding of the Multitudes,* (Goleta: Queenship, 2016), 48–52.

amount they had been praying for. This sounded a little odd, but maybe some people from their church had sent the little boy to give them the gift anonymously.

This caught my attention, though, because we were struggling financially too. So I began to pray, "God, why don't you send a little boy to our door with a bag full of money?" The answer he gave me was, "Why don't you go back to school so you can get a better-paying job?" I didn't know any way I could swing that financially, but God worked it out for me. I was able to go to school and eventually graduated with a master's degree in education. Sometimes God will give us the miracle we ask for, but he wants us to participate with him in getting it.

If we take the time to think and pray about it, we can probably find many miracles that God has worked in our lives. But what about those miracles or healings that never seem to have taken place? Some people might become angry with God when a loved one they've been praying for dies. They might wonder why God miraculously heals some people and not others. That's a very good question.

The only answer that can be given is a difficult one to accept: *God knows what he's doing.* In Isaiah 55:8–9 God tells us:

For my thoughts are not your
Thoughts,
nor are your ways my ways
(says the Lord).[50]
For as the heavens are higher
than the earth,
so are my ways higher than
your ways,
My thoughts higher than
your thoughts.

It's never an easy thing watching someone we love die. But it may be a help to view it from the deceased person's perspective. They're not the lifeless body we see lying in the coffin, or the urn of ashes sitting on a table. They are alive in God's presence, and they are experiencing firsthand just how incredibly loved they are by Almighty God! It is an experience of complete acceptance and complete joy![51]

This isn't going to remove the pain of mourning, but it might give some meaning to a loved one's passing. There are many different kinds of miracles

---

50 The translation in the New American Bible says, "Oracle of the Lord."

51 "He will wipe every tear from their eyes, and there will be no more death or mourning, wailing or pain, [for] the old order has passed away" (Revelation 21:4).

we could be praying for. It might be for a good job, a spouse, the conversion of a family member, a terminal illness, success in life, money to pay the bills, and many other requests that we might present to God. Whatever it is, the prayer must always be ended with the phrase: "Yet not my will, but yours be done" (Luke 22:42).

Nonetheless, our job as Christians is to remind others that miracles are possible,[52] pray with them for the miracle, believe with them for the miracle, and help them to see the miracle even if it is not in the way they had expected.

---

52 "For God, all things are possible" (Matthew 19:26).

Questions for Thought and Discussion

Daily Experiencing the Gifts of Power: Healing and Miracles

1. Do you have any questions about healing and miracles?

2. *Briefly* tell us about a miracle that you experienced. This can be a miracle that happened with you or with someone else.

3. Do you think miracles occur as frequently today as in the early Church? If they don't occur as frequently, why do you think this is the case?

4. Do you think we should be able to perform miracles similar to those Jesus did? Why, or why not?

5. What are some miracles we should be able to see in everyday life?

6. Why do you think God would grant a miraculous healing to one person and not to someone else?

7. How would you respond to someone who asked you why God didn't grant them the healing or the miracle they asked for? You want to give them facts and comfort.

CHAPTER 7

Daily Experiencing the Gifts of Revelation: Prophecy, Word of Knowledge, Mental Images, and Discernment of Spirits

There's an old story about St. Joan of Arc, some fact, and some legend. The fact part of the story is that during the early fifteenth century England and France were fighting with each other in what would later be called the Hundred Years' War.

France wasn't doing well in the struggle at the time, until a sixteen-year-old girl, Joan of Arc, began sharing her visions about a French victory. She convinced King Charles VI that her visions were authentic, so he gave her permission to lead his army against the English. Following several victories led by the young saint, the French morale was heightened, which led to their victory over the English.

The legend part is that one day Joan was telling King Charles about a vision she had when the king suddenly cried out, "Joan, you're always telling me about these visions God is giving you! How come he never talks to me? I am, after all, the king of France!" Joan said, "He is talking to you. You're just not listening."

I have heard it said that God is speaking to us twenty-four hours a day, seven days a week. If we believe that God is with us and guiding us, then why would it be so hard to believe that he is always talking to us? The reason we have such trouble listening to God is because there are a multitude of distractions that we allow to get in the way.

Sometimes, however, God will shove his way through the distractions to give us a message he wants us to hear. This is what happens with the gifts of revelation. They are messages that God gives us for our benefit.

One of the ways God can speak to us is through a private revelation. I experienced this once when I was praying about changing jobs. The job I had was very difficult for me, and there was no peace in my heart.

I applied at several different places, but there was one job that seemed to be custom made for me. The interview went great, and I believed it was the answer to my prayer.

A few days later, though, I got a call from the employer telling me they had chosen someone else for the position. I was crushed! Driving to work that morning I cried out to God, "Don't you care that I'm miserable in this job?!" And then I sensed his voice asking me in the depths of my heart, "Do you love me more than you hate your job?"

As soon as I could admit that I did love God more than I hated my job, an incredible peace came over me. It was a peace that carried me through the remaining time I worked there. What I later, discovered, though, was that had I resigned it would have been one of the worst decisions I ever made.[53] God knows what he's doing. So, God can give us a personal message in prayer, or whenever he wants to.

Another way God can speak to us is as a member of a group or community. During the beginning

---

53 I was teaching a secondary special education class and was having a difficult time with it. Had I resigned I might not have ever been hired anywhere again.

of the 2020 Coronavirus pandemic, a friend of mine had a prophecy that he sent to our intercessory prayer group. In the prophecy God said,

> Hear Me My people! Hear the cry of My voice! For I am with you! I am within you and I am upholding you! Do not fear the threat that you see around you! Did I not deliver Daniel in the lion's den? Did I not deliver Shadrach, Meshach, and Abednego in the fiery furnace? As I delivered them in, and I repeat in their afflictions, so I will deliver you in yours!

The purpose of prophecy is to give encouragement and/or exhortation to a group. Another form of prophecy is directed more toward an individual than to a group. It's called the word of knowledge.

My wife Kathy, and I were at a charismatic prayer meeting one night when she received a message from the Lord. The words started coming to her mentally; her heart began pounding rapidly, and despite her desire not to speak, she knew she had to.

She said, "There is someone here thinking of committing suicide. God wants you to know you're not to do it. He wants you to know that he loves you. Give him your life and he will bless you." Kathy was initially embarrassed and afraid she had made a mistake.

After the prayer meeting, though, a lady approached her and said, "That was for me." The reason she had come to the prayer meeting that night was a last-ditch effort to find something worth living for. If she didn't find it at the prayer meeting, she was going to go home and kill herself.

Marcella, a friend of ours, had a similar experience. She was in the waiting room at a local hospital waiting for her daughter to come out of surgery. During her wait she noticed a lady sitting nearby looking sad. Suddenly, she sensed God's voice: "Go tell her that I love her, and that everything's going to be all right." She hesitated at first, but then she responded to what she sensed God telling her to do. As it turned out, this lady had recently lost her father, six months before her husband had died, and she was struggling with arthritis.

She had recently told God that if he didn't soon give her a sign of hope she was going to end it all. But when Marcella gave her God's message she just broke down in tears. It was the very message she needed to hear.

Another time, Marcella was working at a Life in the Spirit Seminar.[54] She suddenly sensed God telling her to speak these words to one of the participants: "God wants you to sing again." Marcella had no idea who this lady was.

After Marcella gave her this message, the lady told her that at one time she was constantly singing. In fact, they had called her, "the Singer" at work. But after her husband died, she sank into such a deep depression that she hadn't sung a note. God was telling her she needed to start singing again. How wonderful that God knows exactly what we need when we need it.

A Catholic charismatic prayer meeting is an ideal place to learn about and practice using the gift of prophecy.[55] Now, by using the word "practice" I'm not saying that everyone has this gift, and we need to practice using it. But if we have a prophetic gift, the best place to learn how to use it is in a place where it is being used. But can someone learn how to use this gift outside of a charismatic prayer meeting? It's possible.

---

54 This is a seminar for people wanting to receive the baptism in the Holy Spirit.

55 The view that no one has all the gifts is pretty well stated by St. Paul in Romans 12:3–8, 1 Corinthians 12:4–10 and 12–31.

Now, while we may not all have the gift of prophecy, we all do have a prophetic gifting through the sacrament of baptism. At our baptism we became priest, prophet, and king. Our prophetic calling is to let others know the mystery of the universe![56]

This isn't a mystery to those who have surrendered their lives to Jesus Christ, but for much of the world it still is a mystery. The mystery is that God is real! He is madly in love with each one of us and he is constantly drawing us to himself! We have been created for God, and it is only in God that we are going to experience the fullness of life we have been created for! Our prophetic message is no matter how bleak a situation may be, there is hope in Jesus Christ!

We also have an insight into future events. Evil is going to increase (CCC 675), but in the end, evil is going to be conquered by Jesus Christ! (Revelation 20:10) Indeed, evil has already been conquered by Jesus Christ through his death on the cross (CCC 672). Our prophetic mission is to invite those who do not know Jesus to be on the winning team!

So, through our baptism we already have a prophetic ministry, although we may not all have the

---

56 See Ephesians 1:7–10.

gift of prophecy. But God is free to speak to us and through us whether he has specifically given us this gift or not.

What is important is being obedient to God. If we sense God speaking his word to us, we need to speak it out. If it is not of God, he or others will let us know. It may result in a momentary embarrassment but are we willing to be embarrassed for Jesus? On the other hand, it could also be God wanting to deliver a message to someone through us.

In speaking prophetically we don't need to say, "THUS SAITH THE LORD!" No matter how confident someone might be in the message they're speaking they could still be wrong. It's best to preface the message with, "This is what I'm sensing from God," or something similar to that. This avoids the temptation for pride, which is one of the easiest ways for the devil to deceive us.

Prefacing a prophecy in this way could give encouragement to those new in using this gift. A fear that people often have with opening up to this gift is that they're wrong. Their fear is it may be a product of their own imagination. Prefacing a prophecy with, "This is what I am sensing," is saying, "I may be wrong, but this is what I believe God is saying." Some may disagree with this, but I think it's a good way of overcoming an initial fear.

God can also give someone a mental image of a message he wants made known. These are different from the visons mentioned by St. Teresa of Avila[57] and St. John of the Cross.[58] The mystical visions mentioned by these two saints are meant specifically for the one receiving them. It is a mystical experience meant for the recipient's spiritual growth. The mental image, on the other hand, is akin to the gift of prophecy. It is a message the Lord means for the community.[59]

One night at our prayer meeting, Patricia, (one of our members) said the Lord had given her a mental image of a huge bonfire. From the bonfire flames were being shot out in different directions. The message she received from this image was the bonfire was symbolic of our praises to God. As we continue to praise God

---

57 St. Teresa of Avila, *The Interior Castle, Book VI,* trans. Kieran Kavanaugh and Otilio Rodriguez. Washington, D.C. ICS Publications. 1980. Chapters 8 and 9.

58 St. John of the Cross, *The Ascent to Mount Carmel, Book 2* trans. Kieran Kavanaugh and Otilio Rodriguez. Washington, D.C. ICS Publications. chapters 16 and 23.

59 St. John of the Cross, *The Ascent to Mount Carmel, Book 3* chapter 30, #2.

the bonfire grew bigger and embers from the bonfire were being sent out all over the city.

One ember might be sent to someone in prison needing to be touched by God. Another ember might be sent out to someone in depression needing a touch of hope. Another flame might be sent out to someone struggling with a temptation to sin. The message to our community was that our praises went beyond our own edification. God was ministering far beyond our walls through them.

We can hear God's voice if we take the time to listen. He might speak to us through our thoughts or dreams. We might hear him speak through reading scripture, hearing a homily, listening to a song, or talking with others.

But sometimes God will give us a message that is meant for our group or for someone else. When this happens, we need to be willing to speak out what God has given us. In 1 Corinthians 14:1 St. Paul tells us to "strive eagerly for the spiritual gifts, above all that you may prophesy" (NAB).

As I mentioned before, one of the best places to learn how to use the various forms of prophecy is at a Catholic charismatic prayer meeting. The reason for this is because prophecy will not often be seen outside of this venue.

Once we get a sense of how prophecy, the word of knowledge, and mental images can be used, and how God may be speaking through us, we can take this gift into the marketplace. After all, God's intention for the gifts of the Holy Spirit is to continue Jesus's ministry in the world.

Discernment of Spirits

One more gift I want to mention is the discernment of spirits. In 1 Peter 5:8 we're told, "Be sober and vigilant. Your opponent the devil is prowling around like a roaring lion looking for someone to devour." This text will come up again in the chapter on spiritual warfare. As was mentioned earlier in chapter 5, the discernment of spirits is a sense that something isn't right. Whether it's with a person, a situation, or a decision being made there is the awareness that something just isn't right. There might even be the sense of evil being present.

One day my wife and I entered into a bookstore and she suddenly became aware of the presence of evil. Then she saw a sign directing people to a room to have their fortunes told. That is what was causing her to sense the presence of evil. The Church firmly states that we are not to have anything to do with fortunetelling or anything claiming to have knowledge of future events (CCC 2116–2117). This will be discussed more in chapter 10.

Kathy's peace began to decrease even more when she saw a lady enter the room. A sense of urgency came over her and she would not leave the store until she had spoken with the lady. Once the lady left the room Kathy approached her and said, "You don't need to go to a fortune teller. God loves you very much, and if you give your life to him he'll take care of you." The lady thanked her and walked off.

The conversation didn't go any further, but a seed was planted. What is important is that Kathy did what she sensed she had to do because of the evil she was sensing in her spirit. Some people might not go as far as Kathy did, but they will at least know to pray for that person or situation.

Another example of discernment of spirits took place at a business where a friend of mine had applied for a job. He was later offered the job but declined to accept it because he could sense something evil in the establishment. He later found out it was run by

Satanists. The discernment of spirits can also help us in dealing with people and situations in everyday life.

We may have an opportunity to do business with someone that we just don't feel good about. It doesn't mean that person is a Satanist, but God is just trying to keep us out of a bad situation. But the discernment of spirits can also help us to move into a good situation. I have heard of people, who knew they were supposed to marry a certain person.

Any decision of this magnitude, though, needs to be coupled with additional discernment. There's an old story that may or may not be true about Paul McCartney. In the early days of Beatlemania a woman approached him and said, "God told me that we're supposed to be married." He responded with, "But God hasn't told me anything about it."

St. Ignatius of Loyola has a whole section in the Spiritual Exercises on rules for discernment.[60] Suffice it to say that seeking a spiritual director, or a spiritual friend [61] is helpful when making a significant life

---

60 Spiritual Exercises of St. Ignatius of Loyola #169–189 and 313–370 are especially concerned with discernment.

61 The spiritual friend is someone you trust sharing your spirituality with. Their job is not to tell you what to do but to co-discern God's voice speaking to you.

decision. But the peace that can come with the discernment of spirits can also be useful in guiding us in a certain direction. When I was in formation for the diaconate the formation director would often say things like, "You're not deacons yet!"

The insinuation was that we could be asked to leave formation at a moment's notice. I think some of the men were intimidated by this, but I knew in my heart it was God's will for me to be a deacon. I sometimes felt like saying, "If God wants me to be a deacon there's nothing you're going to do about it!" Of course, had I actually said that I might have discovered differently.[62]

---

62 "Jesus answered him, "Again it is written, 'You shall not put the Lord, your God, to the test' " (Matthew 4:7).

Questions for Thought and Discussion

Daily Experiencing the Gifts of Revelation: Prophecy, Word of Knowledge, Mental Images, and Discernment of Spirits

1. Do you have any questions about the gifts of revelation?

2. Briefly describe a time that God has spoken to you. What was the message? How did you respond to it?

3. Describe a situation when you wanted to hear God's voice but were unable to. In what ways were you seeking to hear his voice??

4. Although God may speak to us about major situations, can we also expect him to speak to us about trivialities? Why or why not? Give some examples.

5. What do you think is required of us to hear God's voice?

6. How can you discern if a message is from God or not?

7. What will happen if you give a message to someone or a group and it's not of the Lord?

CHAPTER 8

Daily Experiencing the Gifts of Service: Mercy, Hospitality, Giving, Leadership, and Serving in Ministry

Several years ago, a Christian I was working with told me that one of his gifts was the ability to identify gifts in others. That's not one of the gifts mentioned by St. Paul, but I can see how it may be one of the unmentioned gifts of the Holy Spirit. Some people do need to be pushed in the direction God may be calling them in. One of the attributes I admire in some pastors is their ability to discern, and to call out the gifts they see in the members of their flock.

In any case, when I asked him what my gift was, he said "Mercy." That is not what I wanted to hear. I was hoping he would tell me I had an untapped gift for performing miracles or healing. I apparently wanted a gift that was going to bring me some glory. But personal glory is not the purpose of

> The purpose of the gift of serving is to humbly minister behind the scenes.

the gifts of the Holy Spirit, and this is especially true with the "service gifts." Their purpose is to humbly serve behind the scenes.

So, what are these gifts of service? The Bible gives several examples of what the service gifts are: serving in ministry (Romans 12:7), giving (Romans 12:8), encouragement (Romans 12:8), leadership (Romans 12:8), mercy (Romans 12:8), hospitality (1 Peter 4:9), and intercessory prayer (Ephesians 6:18). Rather than being separate gifts, though, they are all different parts of the same thing. They are all helping gifts, and many of them work in sync with each other.

Let me introduce you to Nestor and Nellie Baca. They had just returned from a pilgrimage to Medjugorje when they felt a strong calling to give something back to God. They had both been successful realtors, had made a lot of money, and began to question the need to make more. So, after a year and a half of prayer they decided to see if there was some way they could serve in Mexico.

Eventually they got involved with the Lord's Ranch in El Paso, Texas. (This is the community that Fr. Rick Thomas, S.J., was a part of.) At the Lord's Ranch, Nestor and Nellie started meeting with the prayer group and participating in their various ministries. The prayer group was called *Las Alas* (the Wings). Through this group they were involved with the prison ministry, prayer at the abortorium, the distribution of food, and other ministries.

One day, as a part of the distribution of food ministry, they met an elderly lady who lived in Juarez. She lived in a ramshackle house made of cardboard and pieces of wood. They were deplored by the condition they saw her living in. When they saw that many people in Juarez were living in houses like this, they realized they had to do something about it. So, they got people together and started building houses for them. To this date they have built at least seventy homes.

They also noticed beggars under a bridge in Juarez who looked very thirsty and hungry. So, they started bringing them bottles of water and passing out bags of lunches. Then when they returned to Albuquerque (they still had a home here) they contacted the Roadrunner food bank and started distributing food once a month from the St. Therese parish gym.

They still minister from time to time in Juarez, and they have been doing this for over twenty years now. This is just one example of the gift of service. Those with this gift will tell Jesus, "You have given so much to me, now what can I do for you?" This is true for any of us. If we take the time to focus on our blessings rather than what we do not have, we'll discover that we have been abundantly blessed!

We have all been called to give to a certain degree, but the gifted giver is one who has a special calling for it. The Holy Spirit compels

> Jesus, you have given so much to me, now what can I do for you?

them to give. The one thing that is obvious about the service gifts is their similarity to each other. A person with the gift of service will usually have a gift of encouragement, giving, leadership, hospitality, and mercy.

This can easily be seen with Nestor and Nellie Baca. Their compassion for the poor in Juarez (mercy) caused them to organize people to help build homes (leadership), requiring them to give and receive donations (giving) and mobilize a system of other helpers. This is evangelization. In doing this they often invited people to stay with them at their home in El Paso (hospitality). This all came from a gift of service.

Those with the gift of service are often doing random acts of kindness. Whenever they see a need they respond to it. They let people go in front of them in a long line at a store. They pay the difference when a customer is short of cash. They're the first to volunteer, and they rarely complain about the work needing to be done. Their servant antennae are always extended, surveying the ground for a need to be met.

Of course, this can develop into a problem too. Some servants become so active with new projects their former commitments suffer from it. They can also burn themselves out. Someone with the gift of service needs to monitor their activities and learn how to *"Just say no!"* But if this gift is in control it is one of the most important gifts of the Holy Spirit in the church today.

When someone sees a member of the Church doing random acts of kindness they begin to wonder what it is about that person that

> Acts of service for a Christian are visible expressions of Jesus's presence.

makes them so different. This can also happen when the observer is not aware of the servant's faith. Their questioning will enable them to hear God's voice more clearly when he speaks to them through their conscience.

The gift of service is a powerful source of evangelization, especially in a secular-oriented world. People hear televangelists boast about the love of God and how faith in Jesus can change their lives. But when they see members of the Church acting no differently than they do it's a hard argument to sell. But what the Christian servant shows the secular world is that there is a difference.

Intercessory Prayer

One gift that is not included in any of St. Paul's lists but should be is the gift of intercessory prayer. We often see prayer as being an individual communing with God for ourselves. Through meditation, perseverance, and silence we are drawn into a more intimate relationship with God. This is all true.

But when we pray for and with others our intercession becomes an indispensable act of service. Its importance lies in the fact that many ministries and individuals are surviving only by someone's prayerful support.

A leader, for instance, can call a group to action, but it is the Holy Spirit who will ignite the fire within them. This comes from prayer. People might think that serving in a particular way is a good idea, but it is the Holy Spirit who is going to motivate them to act. This comes from prayer. Someone might be extremely limited in their resources, but prayer will enable them to feed the multitudes.

One of the problems with the Church today is there are not enough intercessors. In Isaiah 59:16 God looked upon the earth and was appalled that he couldn't find a single intercessor. Now, while there are several intercessors in our Church today, are there enough? Could God be calling you to be an intercessor?

An intercessor is one who hungers and thirsts to pray for the needs of others because they know God answers prayer. If this desire to pray for others is not already in our hearts we can ask God to grant it to us. If we can see the need for this gift then it is a sign we may already have it. The next step is to start praying.

Intercessory prayer can also be done by offering to God our suffering and sacrifices. In Colossians 1:24 St. Paul tells us, "Now I rejoice in my sufferings for your sake, and in my flesh I am filling up what is lacking in the afflictions of Christ on behalf of his body, which is the church" (NAB). What this means is that we each have the opportunity to share in the salvation of the world by uniting our suffering with that of Jesus Christ.[63]

Now, I personally believe that when we unite our sufferings with Jesus's for others we not only contribute to their spiritual benefit, but also to the alleviation of their suffering. This is true whether the healing is physical, psychological, financial, relational, or what have you. I believe Jesus is going to be more apt to answer a request made through suffering because it is a request made with great love and sacrifice.

A few years ago, for instance, I had a bad case of double pneumonia. I was constantly coughing, had trouble sleeping, and it was hard for me to breathe. So, I offered it up for a friend who had a rare form of cancer. He is completely healed from cancer at this time. I know that several other people were praying for him as well but I am confident that in some way God did answer my prayer. Furthermore, it gave meaning to the suffering I was going through.

---

63 This point is confirmed by Pope John Paul II, in the apostolic letter, "Salvifici Doloris: On the Christian Meaning of Human Suffering," (February 11, 1984), #19 Vatican website.

Another example of someone offering their suffering for others was St. Maria Faustina Kowalska (1905–1938). Jesus had revealed to her that her suffering would benefit others (#67). [These references are taken from her *Diary*] On one occasion there was a young lady who was being tempted to commit suicide. Sr. Kowalska was praying for this student when suddenly the saint became quite ill.

Sr. Faustina suffered tremendously for a week and then suddenly the suffering was gone. It ended at the exact time the student was freed from the desire to kill herself. St. Faustina attributed the student's emotional healing to the offering of her suffering (#192).

As we share in Christ's suffering for others we will discover that "suffering is present in the world in order to release love, in order to give birth to works of love toward neighbor, [and] in order to transform the whole of human civilization into a 'civilization of love.' "[64]

Offering our suffering for others and all the gifts of service are about doing acts of love for Jesus.[65]

---

64 John Paul 11, *Salvifici Doloris.* 1984. Vatican Website. February 11, 1984. #30.

65 "Amen, I say to you, whatever you did for one of these least brothers of mine, you did for me" (Matthew 25:40).

Questions for Thought and Discussion

Daily Experiencing the Gifts of Service: Mercy, Hospitality, Giving, Leadership, and Serving in Ministry

1. Do you know someone with the gifts of service? What are some of their attributes you admire and would like to have?

2. In John 13:14 Jesus tells us to wash one another's feet. Give some examples of how this can be done in the real world.

3. In Colossians 1:24 St. Paul says, "Now I rejoice in my sufferings for your sake." How do you think St. Paul, Pope John Paul 11, and St. Faustina found joy in their suffering? Give some examples of how we can find joy in our suffering.

4. The idea of tithing 10 percent of our income to God comes from the word "tithe," which means one-tenth. The first mention of this in scripture is Numbers 14:19–20 when Abram gave Melchizedek a tenth of his booty. Should a Christian be expected to tithe one-tenth of their time, talent, and treasure? Is this a good idea? Why or why not?

5. In the story of the "Widows Mite," (Mark 12:41–44, Luke 21:1–4) Jesus told his disciples that the few pennies the widow put into the treasury were greater than the wealth others had contributed. Why is this a good scripture for talking about the gift of service?

CHAPTER 9

Daily Experiencing the Ephesian 4:11 Gifts: Apostleship, Evangelization, and Pastoring

The gifts mentioned in Ephesians 4:11 are apostles, prophets, evangelists, and pastors. Since I have already dealt with the gift of prophecy and teaching I'll leave these alone. We'll begin, then, with the gift of apostleship. Many people don't think of apostleship as being a gift because they associate it with the twelve apostles. We're not ever going to be one of them. What, then, is the gift of apostleship?

Apostleship is also the first gift St. Paul mentions in 1 Corinthians 12:28. The word itself means, "One who is sent." At face value this can pertain to all followers of Jesus Christ. As I have mentioned elsewhere in the book we are all called to bring Jesus's presence to those we meet in everyday life.

The one with the gift of apostleship, though, is called to "get things started." They recognize a need that isn't being met and they meet that need. An example is someone who begins a missionary activity or plants a church. The idea is they get something new started, form leaders, and then move on. This was typical of what the twelve apostles did, including and especially St. Paul.

But I believe the gift of apostleship can also belong to those who see a need, develop a ministry to meet that need, and stay with it for a while. The LIGHT seminar might be an example of this. The purpose of the seminar is to acquaint on-fire Catholics with a knowledge of the gifts of the Holy Spirit and their use in everyday life. In my interaction with different Catholic groups it seemed like there was a need for this type of ministry.

Another example of apostleship is a program for Catholics who are divorced. A few years ago Jane Zingelman, a Catholic divorcee, couldn't find anything in her area for divorced Catholics. One day she heard Rose Sweet interviewed on the local Catholic radio station. She spoke about a thirteen-week video program that she had developed called *Surviving Divorce.*

When Jane heard Rose speak about her program the Holy Spirit quickened in her heart and she knew this was something that needed to be developed locally. She purchased the video and went through the program herself. Afterward, Jane contacted several parishes to see if any were interested in the program she had developed. Eventually a parish gave her their blessing and she began the *Divorce Recovery Ministry.*

This group meets once a week to view the thirteen videos offered by *Surviving Divorce,* followed with discussion and prayer. This has spun off into two related ministries. The first spin-off is a book club. They each get a book that Jane recommends, read it, and discuss the contents. These are books dealing with relationships, marriage, divorce, spirituality, etc.

Another spin-off is a "meet-up" that is held once a month after Mass. Each participant gets an article on subjects similar to those in the book club. They read the article together and discuss it. All of this has come from Jane recognizing a need in the Church and finding a way to meet that need.

The question we need to ask ourselves is do I see a need in the Church and a way to meet that need? Do I have a gift of apostleship that I'm not using? We're not all called to this, but we need to ask God for the grace to respond to it if we are being called.

Another gift from Ephesians 4:11 is "evangelization." Basically, the gift of evangelization is that hunger in a believer's heart to share the Good News with others. There is a certain level where every Catholic/Christian is commanded to be an evangelist.

In Matthew 28:19 Jesus says, "Go, therefore, and make disciples of all nations, baptizing them in the name of the Father, and of the Son, and of the Holy Spirit, teaching them to observe all that I have commanded you" (NAB). Although this command is often seen as pertaining to the clergy the Church recognizes that all followers of Jesus have a role to play in evangelization (CCC 905–907).

The call to evangelize is further given in 1 Peter 3:15 where we're told, "Always be prepared to give an explanation to anyone who asks you for a reason for your hope, but do it with gentleness and reverence..." This is speaking to all followers of Jesus Christ. This doesn't mean that we all have to be witnessing door to door, passing out tracts in the mall or preaching on the street corner. There is a place for this but not everyone is called to it. Even though we are all called to share our faith with others, there are those who have a special gift for this.

One of these was a friend of mine named John Fidel. John has gone home to be with the Lord now but in the years that I knew him he was a textbook example of someone with the gift of evangelization. Frequently we would have breakfast or lunch together at a restaurant. We would often be sharing something about Jesus, the Church, and the gifts of the Holy Spirit.

On several occasions people came over to our table with questions, wanting to know more about our faith in Jesus Christ. Immediately John would start witnessing to them with gentleness and respect. Often he would end up praying with them. One time we were standing in line at a cafeteria. While I was deciding whether to have fish or Salisbury steak I glanced over at John and saw that he was sharing Jesus with the lady standing next to him.

Another time John was working out in the gym when he saw a lady looking rather despondent leaning against a pillar. Her name was Betty Braswell. John approached her and said, "Do you think you can push over that pillar?" Betty told him she was sure the pillar would hold her and her frustrations up very well. John asked, "What frustrations? Let's take a walk."

John and Betty had never met each other before.

As they walked around the interior of the gym John asked Betty if she knew that Jesus lived in her heart. Since this is what she had been taught in her Catholic faith she told John of course she knew this. But when John explained that she could experience Jesus's presence and his love for her she said, "This is what I want. How do I get it?"

John told her that Jesus was in her heart already. She just needed to ask Jesus to come to life within her. He prayed with her in the middle of the gym, and she received Jesus in her heart and was filled with an incredible joy. The awareness of God's presence and his love has not left her since.

Now, we won't all have a gift for evangelization at the level that John Fidel did, but we are still called to share our faith with others. And since God has called us to this he has also given us a certain level of this gift that he expects us to use.

The last gift I want to mention from Ephesians 4:11 is that of pastoring. It's logical to assume that this gift will be given to pastors and Church leaders. Nonetheless, this gift can also be given to parents.

In the Decree on the Apostolate of Lay People from the Documents of Vatican II [66] we're told that the family is the "domestic sanctuary of the Church." The parents are responsible to show Jesus's love to their children and bring them up in the faith. Parents often leave the religious instruction of their children up to the Church. The Church reminds parents, though, that, "They are the first to pass on the faith to their children and to educate them in it."[67] Parents can pray with their children, read Bible stories and stories about saints to them, and model Jesus's love. They can model this love in the events of everyday life. They can take them to Mass, discuss religious topics, and encourage the children to grow in their faith.

Parents are in a primary position to model and teach their children about having a relationship with God. If they model for their children at an early age that a relationship with God is important to them it will be important for the children as well. The children might eventually turn from the faith, but they will still have the teaching and the modeling their parents provided. When they are ready to have a relationship with Jesus themselves they will already have a foundation to build on.

---

66 Vatican II, *The Decree on the Apostolate of Lay People* (November 18, 1965) #11, Vatican website.
67 Vatican II, #11.

When I was growing up it was my mom who responded to this gift of pastoring. She prayed with me at bedtime, made sure we always prayed before meals, took us to Mass regularly, and sent me to Catholic school from the first through the eighth grades. Since my dad wasn't very religious it was my mom who ensured our faith was provided for. My dad never opposed her in this, but he would not have provided for us spiritually himself.

Just prior to my eighth-grade year my parents were divorced and the man my mom married was a non-practicing Methodist. He saw no reason for practicing his own faith, let alone becoming Catholic. My mom was no longer practicing our faith nor was I. I was also going through some emotional problems and was not finding the answers I was seeking for in the Church. About six years later, though, I met Jesus through the Catholic Charismatic Renewal, and everything I learned from my mom's spiritual pastoring all came back to me. It all began to make sense now.

For a while it might have seemed like all my mom's efforts had gone down the tubes. But she had laid the foundation for me that God is real and a relationship with him is important. This is what a domestic pastor does. The children might still leave the Church, but the parents have left a foundation that will always be a part of their lives.

Parenting in the domestic Church is one of the ways the gift of pastoring can function in everyday life. Any leader in the Church can use the gift of pastoring. Although leaders will have this gift at differing levels, what is important is for pastors in whatever function to put this gift to use.

The way we do this is by becoming an ambassador for Jesus Christ[68] to the flock we are called to serve. The image of a pastor is a shepherd taking care of his or her flock and the ultimate shepherd is Jesus Christ. Therefore, the job of one with the gift of being a pastor is not to lead the flock themselves, but to allow Jesus to shepherd *his* flock through them. How can one do this? By growing in sensitivity to the Holy Spirit.

---

68 "So we are ambassadors for Christ, as if God were appealing through us. We implore you on behalf of Christ, be reconciled to God" (2 Corinthians 5:20).

Questions for Thought and Discussion

For Daily Experiencing the Ephesian 4:11 Gifts:
Apostleship, Evangelization, and Pastoring

1. Name someone with the gift of apostleship?
   What did they start? In what way did this meet
   a certain need?

2. If you could start something in the Church today what would it be?

3. How would you define evangelization? Name
   someone you believe has the gift of evangelization.

4. What do you think some of the characteristics
   are of someone with this gift?

5. What are some different ways that someone
   can evangelize?

6. What are some characteristics of a pastor?

7. Do you think a strong leader will always be a
   good pastor? Why or why not?

8. Can you think of other positions or situations that someone could have the gift of pastoring?

9. How could the recognition of the Ephesians 4:11 gifts help someone grow in their gift?

CHAPTER 10

Overcoming Obstacles to Living the Spirit-Filled Life

Many people have gifts of the Holy Spirit they're not even aware of. We've briefly discussed what some of these gifts are and how they can be used in everyday life. Even with this knowledge, though, there are obstacles that need to be overcome for these gifts to come to life within us.

The first obstacle is the belief that God doesn't love us. This might come from a feeling of unworthiness, an awareness of our sins, or doubting that God is powerful enough to personally love everyone in the world. Or someone might believe that God loves them as a member of the human race, but not personally.

This is a problem because if I don't believe God loves me personally, then I'm not going to believe he has personally given me gifts of the Holy Spirit. This is one of Satan's most powerful weapons in keeping Christians from receiving the abundant life God has for us. It is the belief that God is not powerful enough or loving enough to personally care for us.

This is a temptation I was faced with when I was first prayed with to receive the baptism in the Holy Spirit. The first thought that came to me was how unworthy I was to receive this gift. As a result of my negative thinking the only thing I received from that prayer was extreme depression. I believe this was the devil's attempt to get me to turn away from God.

Fortunately, the keynote speaker that night talked about the importance of thanking God in all circumstances. Using Romans 8:28 [69] and 1 Thessalonians 5:18[70] as his guides, he shared how God can turn bad things into good when we praise him for them.

So, later that night I took the speaker's message to heart. I began to praise God and thank him for my depression. I praised and thanked him for not granting me the baptism in the Holy Spirit. I praised and thanked him that I felt unworthy of his love!

---

69 "We know that all things work for good for those who love God, who are called according to his purpose."
70 "In all circumstances give thanks, for this is the will of God for you in Christ Jesus."

And as I continued to praise God out loud, my pretentious praise suddenly became authentic praise, and I began praising God while

> Knowing God loves us is crucial for growing in the Spirit-filled life.

filled with joy! I actually had received the baptism in the Holy Spirit earlier that evening, but the devil was trying to keep it from me. He knew that if he could convince me that I was not loved by God, then he would keep me from receiving this gift God wanted me to have.

We need to believe that God loves us in order for him to be able to work with us. God will still love us whether we believe it or not, but we will not have the spiritual freedom to be used by him. The best way to overcome thoughts of unworthiness is to combat them with God's promises in scripture.

One of the ways this can be done is by reflecting on John 3:16 [71] with a slight change in the wording. Instead of saying, "For God so loved *the world* that he gave his only begotten Son," say, "For God so loved [your name] that he gave his only begotten Son." You

---

71 "For God so loved the world that he gave his only Son, so that everyone who believes in him might not perish but might have eternal life" (NAB).

can also say, "For God so loved *me* that he gave his only begotten Son."

Another good scripture is Jeremiah 29:11–12: "For I know well the plans I have in mind for you [your name], plans for your welfare and not for woe, so as to give you a future of hope" (NAB). If I used Isaiah 43:1–4 for myself it would read:

> But now, thus says the Lord, who created you, *Michael*, and formed you. Do not fear for I have redeemed you, *Michael*, I have called you by name: you are mine. When you pass through the waters, *Michael*, I will be with you; through rivers, you shall not be swept away.
>
> *Michael*, when you walk through fire, you shall not be burned, nor will flames consume you. For I, the Lord, am your God, *Michael*, I am the holy one. *Michael*, I give Egypt as a ransom for you, Ethiopia and Seba in exchange for you, because you, *Michael*, are precious in my sight and honored, and I love you" (adapted from NAB).

The idea is to take a promise of God and read it as addressed to you personally. Jesus used scripture when he was tempted by Satan and we should too.

Shortly after my conversion I was still struggling with deep-seated feelings of inferiority. (Heck, to a certain degree I still struggle with them.) But when I was nineteen to twenty years old I was really having a struggle with it. I didn't feel like I was worthy to receive any of the gifts of the Holy Spirit, or to be used by God.

One night at a prayer meeting a lady had a prophecy that I felt was meant specifically for me. She said, "How dare you say that you're not worthy! I sent my Son to die for you to make you worthy! How dare you say that you're not worthy!" That prophecy has stuck with me all my life long. While it is true that none of us are worthy of God's love in ourselves, it is through Jesus Christ that we have been made worthy.

Another area that can affect us spirituality is dabbling in the occult. The occult is anything that claims to have supernatural power apart from God. Examples of this are: astrology, fortune telling, tarot cards, Ouija board, horoscopes, witchcraft, Reiki (or supernatural healing apart from God), channeling, and so on.

Many people, and even some Christians, claim there's nothing wrong with these. They're either seen as being innocent forms of amusement or something completely separate from our relationship with God.

Some people are just fascinated by their mystique. The Catholic Church, however, completely condemns the occult.

In the Catechism of the Catholic Church #2116 we read:

All forms of divination are to be rejected: recourse to Satan or demons, conjuring up the dead or other practices falsely supposed to "unveil" the future, consulting horoscopes, astrology, palm reading, interpretation of omens and lots, the phenomena of clairvoyance, and recourse to mediums all conceal a desire for power over time, history, and, in the last analysis, other human beings, as well as a wish to conciliate hidden powers. They contradict the honor, respect, and loving fear that we owe God alone.

Not only are occult practices condemned by the Church because they are false but participating in them can open someone up to demonic influences. In other words, it's saying yes to the devil, and giving him some control of our lives.

For instance, trusting in the stars to guide us through life is saying that we don't trust God in charge of our lives. The devil's job is to get us to place our trust in something else besides God. Some people might initially look at their horoscope out of interest, but they often find that they expect, or hope for the predictions to take place.

It might begin as a simple curiosity, but it can develop into a habit and a belief system. Growing in our faith in God isn't easy, and it becomes even more of a struggle when a distractor is thrown in to cloud our faith. This is the devil's goal with any form of the occult.

In CCC 2117 we're told:

All practices of magic or sorcery, by which one attempts to tame occult powers, so as to place them at one's service and have a supernatural power over others—even if this were for the sake of restoring their health—are gravely contrary to the virtue of religion. These practices are to be even more condemned when accompanied by the intention of harming someone, or when they have recourse to the intervention of demons. Wearing charms is also reprehensible. *Spiritism* often implies divination or magical practices; the Church for her part warns the faithful against it. Recourse to so-called traditional cures does not justify either the invocation of evil powers or the exploitation of another's credulity.

So, what does this all mean? If we want to live the Spirit-filled life, grow in our relationship with God, and stay out of the clutches of the evil one, we absolutely have to stay out of the occult. If we have been involved with the occult, we need to renounce it in Jesus's name, and stay away from it.

One of the ways we can renounce the occult is by reciting our baptismal promises. It never hurts to remind ourselves and the spiritual world of the promises we have made.

Baptismal Promises[72]

Leader: Do you reject Satan?

Response: I do

Leader: And all his works?

Response: I do.

Leader: And all his empty promises?

Response: I do.

---

72 The baptismal promises are taken from the *Rite of Christian Initiation of Adults* New York: Catholic Book Publishing CO. 1988, 157, #C.

Leader: Do you believe in God, the Father Almighty, creator of heaven and earth?

Response: I do.

Leader: Do you believe in Jesus Christ, his only Son, our Lord, who was born of the Virgin Mary, was crucified, died, and was buried, rose from the dead, and is now seated at the right hand of the Father?

Response: I do.

Leader: Do you believe in the Holy Spirit, the holy Catholic Church, the communion of saints, the resurrection of the body, and life everlasting?

Response: I do.

Leader: God, the all-powerful Father of our Lord Jesus Christ, has given us a new birth by water and the Holy Spirit and forgiven all our sins. May he also keep us faithful to our Lord, Jesus Christ for ever and ever. Amen.

Another area we need to cover is clinging to unforgiveness. Jesus tells us, in Matthew 6:14:

If you forgive others their transgressions, your heavenly Father will forgive you. But if you do not forgive others, neither will your Father forgive your transgressions (NAB).

There is a similar text in Mark 11:25:

When you stand to pray, forgive anyone against whom you have a grievance, so that your heavenly Father may in turn forgive you your transgressions (NAB).

Forgiveness, or at least the willingness to forgive, is a <u>VERY BIG DEAL</u> with God! In Matthew 18:21–35 Jesus tells the story about a servant who owed his master a great deal of money. Some translations have this at 10,000 talents of gold or millions of dollars. When his master threatened to sell him and his family to repay the debt the servant pleaded for mercy. Having mercy on his servant the master forgave the entire debt.

> God takes forgiveness very seriously!

The servant later came across another servant owing him a hundred denarii or a few dollars. The servant pleaded with his fellow servant for mercy, but he was given none. Instead, he was put into prison until he paid the entire debt. On hearing what had happened, the master recanted his forgiveness from the first servant and had him put into prison. Jesus finished the story saying, "So will my heavenly Father do to you, unless each of you forgivers his brother from his heart" (NAB).

Jesus has forgiven us all our sins through his death on the cross. It is his free gift to those who will receive it.[73] There is nothing we have done to earn this salvation.[74] But there is the expectation on the part of Jesus Christ that we are going to forgive others as he has forgiven us.

We give God permission to do this when we pray the Our Father: "Forgive us our trespasses as we forgive those who trespass against us." This prayer should give us pause to consider those we have not yet forgiven, because our forgiveness is dependent on it.

It is understandable, of course, that someone may have been hurt so deeply that it seems impossible for them to forgive. But what Jesus does require of us is to at least have the desire to forgive. God can work with that. What God can't work with is someone who has decided they will never forgive the one who has wronged them. Not only will this decision keep them from growing spiritually, it will hurt them physically and psychologically as well.

---

73 "The wages of sin is death, but the gift of God is eternal life in Christ Jesus our Lord" (Romans 6:23).

74 "For by grace you have been saved through faith, and this is not from you, so no one may boast" (Ephesians 2:8–9).

Questions for Thought and Discussion

Overcoming Obstacles for Living a Spirit-Filled Life

1. Besides those obstacles mentioned in this chapter, can you think of other obstacles to growing in the Spirit-filled life? What are they? What can be done to alleviate them?

2. Why do you think it's hard for some people to believe God loves them personally?

3. What can you do to make others aware of God's love for them?

4. What are some things you can do to be more aware of God's love?

5. Why do you think so many people are drawn to the occult these days?

6. Do you think that popular fiction glorifying the occult can be used to teach Christian values? Why or why not? If you believe it can, how would you do this?

7. Why is the recitation of our baptismal promises a good step to take when renouncing the occult?

8. Why do you think forgiveness is so important to God?

9. How can you forgive someone when you still feel hurt by them? What steps can be taken?

CHAPTER 11

The Prayer of Forgiveness

Occasionally it's good to reflect on some instances where there might be a need for forgiveness in our lives. For this reason, we have a prayer of forgiveness to assist with the reflection process. Whether this is done as a group, such as during a L.I.G.H.T. seminar, or individually, the first step is to prayerfully put yourself in the presence of God. Read each text in the reflection slowly pausing at the end of each line, giving time to listen to the Holy Spirit.

Not every line of text will address an area needing your forgiveness. If you do come to an area where you recognize the need for forgiveness, stay there with the Lord. Call to mind the person and the instance needing to be forgiven and then say, "I forgive **[name]** for **[name what they did that needs your forgiveness]** in Jesus's name. If you can't forgive them then ask for the grace to forgive them. Remember that forgiveness is a choice. You can choose to forgive someone whether you feel like it or not.

Opening Prayer

God, it is my desire to be completely set free from any unforgiveness that I might have in the depths of my heart. Please remind me of any unforgiveness that I might not be aware of and grant me the freedom to forgive those that need to be forgiven.

Forgiving God

Lord, I forgive you for those times you appeared to be absent in my life.

I especially want to forgive you for allowing my loved one(s) to die when I prayed for their healing.

I forgive you for the emptiness their passing made me feel. Help me to know that death is the ultimate healing and that you did answer my prayer.

I forgive you for the poor start I had in life. I was not born in a family of wealth or with many of the advantages that others do.

I forgive you for not granting me these advantages.

I forgive you that I am not as talented or as attractive as I would like to be.

I forgive you for not giving me the opportunities that others have had.

Lord, I forgive you for all my disappointments in life, and for anything else that has caused me to be angry with you.

You are not to blame for any of these, but I have held you responsible for them in my heart.

Grant me the grace to let the anger go, and to be filled with the joy of your forgiveness.

Forgiving Myself

Lord, with your grace, I forgive myself for not taking advantage of the educational and life opportunities that have come to me.

I forgive myself for hurting others, whether intentional or not, and I pray they would receive the grace to forgive me.

I forgive myself for not being a better son, daughter, sister, brother, or friend. I could kick myself for some of the things I said and did.

There were also some things I should have said or done but did not.

I forgive myself for the life choices that didn't turn out so well for me.

Lord, it is especially difficult for me to forgive myself for the times I deliberately turned from you and your love for me. For those times I ask for your forgiveness, and for the grace to forgive myself.

Forgiving Parents

Lord, I want to thank you for my parents. We didn't always see eye to eye, but I want to thank you for them anyway. I know they did the best they could, even though it didn't seem that way at the time. So, I want to take this opportunity to forgive them.

I forgive them for the times they didn't even try to understand me, or the things I was going through. That's how it seemed to me, at least.

I forgive them for the times I was beaten or punished, whether I deserved it or not.

I forgive them for the times they seemed to prefer my brother(s) or sister(s) to me.

I forgive my parents for abandoning me either through divorce, death, being too busy, or pursuing other interests.

I forgive my parents for not encouraging me, taking an interest in my dreams, or showing their love for me.

Forgiving Siblings

Lord, please grant me the grace to forgive my siblings.

It is my desire to forgive the unkind things they said and did to me while we were growing up.

I forgive them for the times they called me names, squealed on me, or stole from me.

I forgive them for the times they abused me or used their strength against me.

I forgive them for getting more ice cream, privileges, or love than I did. This might not have been the way it happened, but it's how I saw it.

I forgive them for not keeping in touch with me.

I forgive them for hurting me physically, emotionally, or spiritually whether they intended to or not.

For any deep-seated hurt that I may not even be aware of now, I forgive them.

Grant them the grace to forgive me for anything I have done to them.

Forgiving Relatives

Lord, I forgive any relatives—uncles, aunts, cousins, nieces, nephews, or grandparents—who have treated me in an unkind or abusive way.

For any unkind words or actions, I forgive them.

I forgive any relative who has hurt my family through lying, cheating, stealing, or taking advantage of our trust.

I forgive them for taking advantage of our generosity.

I forgive them for any inappropriate touching, name calling, or shaming words they said to me.

I forgive them for exposing me to drugs, alcohol, and/or a lifestyle that made me feel uncomfortable.

Lord, for any way I feel my relatives have hurt me I forgive them right now.

Forgiving Friends, Acquaintances, and Coworkers

Lord, I pray for the grace to forgive any friends, acquaintances or coworkers who have hurt me.

I forgive them for the times they stabbed me in the back to improve their position at school, in a group, or with a company.

I forgive them for the times they put me down to give more importance to themselves.

I forgive them for the times they talked behind my back, spread false rumors about me, or tried to ruin my reputation.

I forgive them for bullying me and taking away my peace.

I forgive them for taking something from me because they were jealous of my having it.

I forgive them for any physical or emotional pain they have caused me.

Lord, I thank you for all the good friends, acquaintances, and coworkers I have had. They have been a blessing to me. But it is my desire to forgive each of them who caused pain in my life, or in the lives of those who are dear to me.

If I am having trouble granting any one of them forgiveness for something they either did to me, or are doing right now, I pray for the grace to be set free to forgive them from my heart.

I forgive those who have spoken against me or persecuted me in any way for my religious beliefs.

Forgiving Teachers

Lord, God, I thank you for all the good teachers I've had. They have truly been a blessing to me. But I also want to take this opportunity to forgive those teachers who were less than helpful to me.

For those teachers who discouraged me and made me feel like a failure, I forgive them, Lord.

I forgive any teacher for putting me in a low academic group, making me feel stupid.

I forgive those teachers who punished me when I didn't do anything wrong. Sometimes they wouldn't even let me defend myself. I do forgive them, Lord.

I forgive those teachers who were constantly yelling, making school an unpleasant experience.

I forgive those teachers who were boring, silly, or really didn't teach me anything.

I forgive those teachers who made me feel uncomfortable with an inappropriate touch or comment.

I forgive those teachers who punished me in a demeaning way in front of the class.

Lord, I forgive any teacher throughout my earliest to my highest year in school who hurt me in any way at all.

Forgiving Church Leadership

Lord, I forgive any priest, deacon, religious education teacher, youth leader, office staff, pastor, or any person affiliated with the church who has hurt me.

For those responsible for boring homilies and long, drawn-out liturgies, I forgive them, Lord.

For those who belittled or talked down to me whenever I asked a question, I forgive them, Lord.

I forgive any church leader who pressured me into doing something I didn't want to do. They destroyed my faith in the church, and in you, my God.

I forgive those church leaders who were too busy to even talk to me.

I forgive those church leaders who were not good models of their faith, causing me to question, or even to lose, my own faith.

I forgive those church leaders who lost their temper and yelled at me over the phone, or in person.

I forgive those religious teachers who gave uninspiring and boring classes.

For those representatives of the church who were unkind to others and/or to me personally, I forgive them, Lord.

Please grant me the grace to forgive anyone in the church who has hurt me in any way. It is my desire to forgive them, Lord. Please grant me the grace to forgive them from my heart.

Forgiving Spouses

Lord, I forgive my spouse for the times he/she was impatient with me or wouldn't listen to what I was trying to tell him/her.

I forgive my spouse for trying to punish me with the silent treatment.

I forgive my spouse for not always agreeing with me.

I forgive my spouse for any lack of commitment, showing of love, or giving me encouragement.

I forgive my spouse for leaving me through separation, divorce, or death.

Lord, I forgive my spouse for spending more quality time with others, or their own interests, than with me and/or the family.

I forgive my spouse for wanting to argue more than to listen.

I forgive my spouse for the mean things he/she has said and/or done to me.

I forgive my spouse for being different than when we were first married.

I forgive my spouse for not taking more of an interest in the upkeep of the home and family.

Lord, I forgive my spouse for any anger I have for her/him at this time.

I ask you for the grace to truly forgive [name] from my heart, and I pray [name] would receive the grace to forgive me as well.

Forgiving Others

I forgive any bosses who treated me unfairly, wouldn't give me credit for the good work I did, and only criticized the mistakes I made.

I forgive them for not giving me the promotion I deserved, not giving me a raise, and keeping me from advancing.

I forgive any doctors for their misdiagnosis. I forgive them for not having a good bedside manner.

I forgive those doctors who did not do enough for my loved one(s).

I forgive any lawyer(s), who either did not do a good job of representing me or found ways to hurt me as much as they possibly could.

I forgive anyone who has sued me.

I forgive anyone who hurt me, resulting in a court case.

I forgive any law enforcement personnel for treating me rougher than I deserved.

I forgive any criminal who has hurt me or those that I love.

I forgive my neighbors for not being as considerate as they should be.

I forgive those drivers who have cut me off in traffic, made obscene gestures, or ran me off the road. I forgive that driver who ran into my car, causing an accident.

I forgive the drunk or reckless driver who caused the death of my loved one(s).

I forgive the computer tech who sent the virus that crashed my computer.

I forgive the person who stole my identity, withdrawing money from my bank account.

Summary Prayer

Lord, I choose right now to forgive anyone I have yet to forgive. And if I am not able to forgive them right now, I pray for the grace to be able to forgive them in the near future. If I have no desire to forgive them, I ask you for the grace to have this desire. It is my desire to serve you, God, and if my unforgiveness is going to keep me from this then I want to be able to forgive. I pray this in Jesus's name. Amen.

CHAPTER 12

Daily Growing in the Spirit-Filled Life

Some people think that when they've received their sacraments, been prayed-with to receive the release of the Holy Spirit or surrendered their lives to Jesus Christ there's nothing more out there. They think there's nothing more they have to give to God, or that God has to give to them. The next step is heaven, or purgatory, or whatever the afterlife holds.

The truth, however, is that this is only the beginning of what God has prepared for us! What God wants us to do for him after we've received these blessings is to make our hearts docile to the Holy Spirit. He wants us to give him free reign to work in us and through us.

I like to compare this to uniting ourselves with Jesus on the cross. St. Paul tells us in Romans 6:6, "We know that our old self was crucified with him, so that our sinful body might be done away with, that we might no longer be in slavery to sin" (NAB). As Jesus's body was crucified and put to death on the cross, so must our sinful habits be crucified and put to death. Rest assured I am not talking about making ourselves holy. Only God can do that. But we can cooperate with God's grace in becoming the people he has created us to be.

So, at the top of the image of a crucifix is Jesus's head, still wearing the crown of thorns. One of the first things we need to be crucified of is our thought life. In the book of Ephesians, we're told:

> Put away the old self of your former way of life, corrupted through deceitful desires, and be renewed in the spirit of your minds, and put on the new self, created in God's way in righteousness and holiness of truth (Eph. 4:22–24, NAB).

At the top of the crucifix with Jesus's head we need to delete the thinking of our former lives and replace it with "the mind of Christ" (1 Corinthians 2:16b). I call this "mental overwrite." We delete our former way of thinking by replacing it with a new way of thinking.

Mental Overwrite

One of the first ways we can do this is to start reading scripture. This should be done on a daily basis. With our busy lifestyles it's best to schedule a daily appointment with God. This schedule may change from time to time, but our appointment with God should be important enough that we won't let it go altogether. And even if we do miss a day or two, this is not the unforgiveable sin. What we want to do is develop a habit of prioritizing the reading of God's Word in our lives.

Scripture can be looked at as being God's love letter to each one of us. It is God letting us know who he is, who we are, and how we can live an abundant life. Surely, this is an important bit of information to find out from our creator!

Scripture also helps us to know who Jesus is. After all, "He is the image of the unseen God" (Colossians 1:15, NAB). As we come to know Jesus Christ through reading scripture, we will come to know the God of the universe! The only way we can have a relationship with anyone is by getting to know them. Reading scripture helps us to know who the Father, the Son, and the Holy Spirit are, and what this should mean to us personally.

In reading the New Testament we can also get to know who we are through

> The Bible is a love letter from God.

Jesus Christ. We are adopted children of God.[75] Through Jesus Christ we can call the Father "our Dad!"[76] There is an intimate bond we have with him. The secular world, on the other hand, has given us the image of ourselves as being insignificant. We have to earn being loved by reaching certain standards the culture has created for us.

But God loves us exactly as we are. We have each been created with dignity, worth, and the potential for greatness. As we read scripture and choose to believe what it says, the secular world's view is overwritten and deleted from our memories.

This can also take place when we read the spiritual masters of our faith, like St. John of the Cross, St. Teresa of Avila, St. Therese of the Infant Jesus, and other saints. We can get this from reading contemporary spiritual writers. We can get this from reading the daily texts for Mass from a Missal. The point is to overwrite the false image of ourselves and replace it with God's image.

---

75 Ephesians 1:4b–5.
76 Romans 8:15.

Making Tracks with Our Feet

From the head of Jesus, we move down to his feet nailed to the cross. Jesus once used his feet to move around the countryside, ministering to the needs of others. Our feet often move about in search of meeting their own needs. They ask, "What is it that will give me pleasure, fulfillment and satisfaction?"

But Jesus's feet moved to wash the feet of others. So, as our feet are nailed to the cross with those of Jesus, we will begin to die to the constant need for self-preservation and begin to recognize the needs of others. We will begin to sense a desire, like St. Mother Teresa of Calcutta, to quench the thirst of Jesus by serving others.[77]

But we don't have to wait for this desire to come bubbling forth in our hearts. We can begin serving be-

> **We need to serve as Jesus served.**

cause Jesus has commanded it of us,[78] and we want to be obedient to him. Sometimes, we can get a good

---

77 Reference is made to Mother Teresa's thoughts on "quenching the thirst of Jesus" in, *Come Be My Light: The Private Writings of the Saint of Calcutta,* P. 41.

78 Some examples of this can be seen in Matthew 20:26, 25:31–46, Mark 10:43, Luke 10:29–37, and John 15:1–15.

feeling from serving others, but this shouldn't be our primary motive. We serve because if we love God, we will in fact love others.[79]

This doesn't mean we're necessarily going to feel love for them, or that we're going to feel like serving. But it does mean we have made a commitment to love and a commitment to serve. Jesus didn't go to the cross because he thought it was going to feel good. He did it because he made a choice to love us and be obedient to his Father.

When our feet are nailed to the cross with Jesus's feet, we're going to love and serve for the same reason. The important thing about serving is to keep our intention clear. If we're doing it to ensure a high place in heaven or to make ourselves holy, then we're doing it for the wrong reason.

We serve because we have nailed our feet to Jesus's feet on the cross. In doing so we have made a commitment to continue his work of service. As we choose to serve others we are quenching the thirst of Jesus Christ.

---

79 "If anyone says, 'I love God,' but hates his brother, he is a liar; for whoever does not love a brother whom he has seen cannot love God whom he has not seen" (1 John 4:20).

The Right Hand of Fellowship

We move now from Jesus's feet on the cross to his right hand nailed through the wrist. This is the hand of community. Whenever someone is asked to take an oath, make a pledge, or shake hands with someone it's done with the right hand. There are several places in scripture that mention Jesus sitting at God's right hand as being a special place of honor. So, we can look at Jesus's right hand nailed to the cross as being the hand of fellowship and community.

In community and fellowship, we're telling others they are more important than we are. In Philippians 2:3–4 we're told: "Do nothing from selfishness or conceit, but in humility count others better than yourselves. Let each of you look not only to his own interests, but also to the interests of others" (RSV).

> We need to recognize our need for each other.

Where our tendency is to put ourselves first, Christian fellowship demands that we put others first. But we don't do it because they need us, and we have something that can benefit them. We do it, rather, because we need them. The ideal community is where the members are aware of their need for each other. This is the idea of community St. Paul gives in Romans 12: 4–8, and 1 Corinthians 12:14–31. We are all members of the body of Christ, and we need each other.

In the Roman Catholic tradition, community has often been seen as attending Mass. This is theologically correct! At Mass, the body of Christ comes together to worship God as "one," to receive Jesus through the Eucharist, and to take Jesus out to the rest of the world. But we are also social beings in need of interacting with each other. We need a medium in which we can share our faith, grow in relationships, and hold each other accountable.

Fortunately, there are various resources for meeting this need. There are Catholic charismatic prayer meetings, ACTS groups, Cursillo groups, Bible studies, the Catholic Daughters, the Legion of Mary, groups specifically for men, groups specifically for women, groups specifically for youth, the Knights of Columbus, and several other groups that provide a source of fellowship for Catholics. These are all good, if the business part of the meeting doesn't overshadow the fellowship.

Catholics need to take advantage of these opportunities and grow in a relationship of spiritual friendship and trust. It's also within the context of a community that we can discover and grow in the gifts God has given us. As we grow in fellowship, our familiarity will make it easier to sense where there is a need, and how the Holy Spirit may be calling us to meet that need.

God wants us to have fellowship with each other, because he wants us to share in the love of the Father, the Son, and the Holy Spirit. The Trinity is a fellowship of love that is so perfect they are one. This is what God is calling us to.[80]

Through the power of the Holy Spirit, God is calling us to live in a fellowship of love with each other. Sin keeps us from this, but as we grow in our fellowship with each other and with Jesus we will begin to experience the kind of fellowship God wants us to have.

Jesus's Praying Hands

On the other side of the cross is Jesus's left hand. Many times, before Jesus was crucified, his left hand

---

80 "That they may all be one, as you, Father, are in me and I in you, that they also may be in us, that the world may believe that you sent me" (John 17:20).

would be joined with his right when he went to his Father in prayer. Prayer was important for Jesus, and we can see in scripture where he went off by himself to be alone with the Father.[81] If Jesus himself felt the need for prayer, surely we need it even more.

Prayer is essential to the spiritual life because it keeps us in touch with God, who is our power source. It reminds us that God is always present and, if we take the time to listen, will enable us to hear his voice more clearly.

At rock bottom, prayer is simply talking with God. Note that prayer is not just talking to God, it's talking with God. Too often prayer is seen as something we do rather than something we participate in. When we share something of ourselves with God, we need to listen to him respond. This is how we grow in our relationship with God. We share ourselves with him, and he shares himself with us. This is basically what prayer is all about

Although there are many different types of prayer, the most basic form is called spontaneous prayer. This is prayer that springs from the depths of the heart.

---

81 For instance: Mark 1:35, Matthew 14:23, Luke 6:12, Luke 22:41–44, John 12:27–28, John 11:41–42.

Whether someone is immediately in need of God's presence or offering their day to him, spontaneous prayer expresses our specific intentions to him. It encourages the one praying to reflect on what they want to say and put their thoughts into words.

Prayers that have been prewritten or memorized are very good too, provided the words are prayed and not just recited. It's very easy just to recite the words with a prayer we're quite familiar with. The words are said but the mind is somewhere else. When this happens, the worst thing we can do is get angry and start condemning ourselves for it.

One way of responding to the distractions is to remind ourselves of the one to whom we're praying and move on.[82] Vocal prayers recited in this way can lead to deeper levels of prayer, so there's nothing wrong with them at all.

But spontaneous prayer is like having a conversation with a friend. It's sharing ourselves with God and listening to God share himself with us. For those who might not have a whole lot to say, though, it's going to

---

82 This is the suggestion given by St. Teresa of Avila on praying the Our Father in chapter 24, #5 of *The Way of Perfection*. This can also be applied to any vocal prayer.

make for a very short prayer: "Hi, God, this is Deacon Mike. We'll see you tomorrow." That might be a bit of an exaggeration, but there is a guide for praying spontaneously. It's a prayer outline called ACTS.

The letter A is for

Adoration

After taking a moment to still our minds and be aware that God is truly present with us we begin with adoration. This is simply praising God: "God, I praise you, I love you, I worship you, I adore you! You are everything to me! Help me to surrender my life more fully to you! God, you are the king of kings and the lord of lords. The entire universe is in your hands! I praise you for my family and all the wonderful things you've given to me!"

Remember that praise and worship is one of the purposes for the gift of tongues. This is a good place for its use if one desires. It's praising God for the wonders of creation, the wonder of his love, and the wonder of his awesome power! In Psalm 22:3 we're told: "Yet thou art holy, enthroned on the praises of Israel" (RSV). This is often interpreted as saying that God is present in the praises of his people. As we adore and worship God with our praises, we can begin to sense his presence within us. Adoration is an awesome way to begin a prayer.

The C is for

Contrition

We call to mind our sins and ask Jesus for forgiveness. Instead of just listing our sins, though, we need to talk them over with Jesus. Ask him to help you understand why some sins are committed over and over again. Can you make a plan for avoiding these sins, such as staying away from people and situations that draw you into their grasp? Are there things you can do to strengthen your determination not to sin? And if you're asking for Jesus's forgiveness, have you forgiven others or asked them to forgive you?

In addition to those sins we have committed through our actions, we can also be guilty of committing sin by not doing something. These are called "sins of omission." Not saying our daily prayers, not helping someone in need, or avoiding an opportunity to serve are examples of sins of omission. We need to remember these sins as well when confessing our sins to Jesus. Of course, this does not replace the sacrament of reconciliation. Its purpose here is to call to mind and confess our sins before we can get to confession.

In summary, then, these are some points of conversation between you and Jesus that can come up with the prayer of contrition.[83]

The *T* is for

Thanksgiving

In this prayer we thank God for all the gifts he's given us. We can thank him for the day, the sunset, our health, our families, creation, our job, our faith, and on and on. We can also be thankful for some of the things we gave him adoration for as well. But it's also important that we don't leave out those situations and circumstances that we're not completely overjoyed about. In 1 Thessalonians 5:18 we're told: "In all circumstances give thanks, for this is the will of God for you in Christ Jesus" (NAB).

This doesn't mean God wills bad things to happen to us. God's will for us, rather, is to praise him *in all*

---

83 This is similar to the General Examination of Conscience outlined by St. Ignatius of Loyola #24–43 of the Spiritual Exercises.

circumstances. When bad things happen to us, we can still praise God! We praise him because he is God.

We praise him because we know that he still loves us and is in control of our lives. We praise him because we know that in spite of the situation or circumstance we're in, "With God all things are possible!" (Matthew 19:26). And finally, we praise God because, "We know that all things work for good for those who love God" (Romans 8:28, NAB).

We might not *feel* this level of thanksgiving, but we thank God anyway to keep our faith from crumbling. We thank God because it is by trusting in him that our faith will be strengthened! We thank God because, whether we can understand it or not, it is what God has commanded us to do.

The S is for

Supplication

This can also be called a prayer of petition. It is in this part of the prayer that we make our requests to God. This can be a prayer for ourselves, for someone else, or for a situation we're concerned about. God, of course, is aware of our needs and what we're going to pray even before we ask him. But God wants us to ask so we'll praise him when he grants us our requests.

In Luke 18:1–8 Jesus tells a story about a widow who came to an unjust judge to give her a decision against her adversary. Initially, the unjust judge wasn't going to do anything about it. He had no concern for the feelings of others or of the wrath of God. But because of the lady's persistence he finally gave in to her request.

Jesus's point was that God will surely hear and answer all our prayers. But there are many who will claim that God has never answered their prayers. How can this be the case? Either God does answer prayer, or he doesn't.

The problem is that when we pray we are looking at one microscopic part of our lives, whereas God sees the whole thing. He's looking at the whole of who we are: past, present, and to come. God doesn't will for evil, bad, or inconvenient things to happen to us. This is the fault of sin and free will. But God can work for good even in trials.

And sometimes, God is calling us to participate with him in answering our prayer. In a previous chapter I asked God to provide for our financial need like he had provided for the lady we interviewed on the radio. God's response to me was to finish college so I could get a better job. Sometimes God will give us what we ask for by having us do something about it.

There are also those times when we cannot understand why God doesn't answer prayer in a specific way. It's in these times we're called to put our trust in him and give our faith the chance to grow. It's the same when we pray for others, local, national, and/or world situations. We never know the effect our prayers are going to have on what we're praying for, but we know that God is faithful in answering our prayers.[84] The important thing is to pray and to never give up on prayer.

These four ways of being crucified with Christ can help us grow in the Spirit-filled life and an openness to the gifts God has given us. If we're not used to practicing these spiritual disciplines, getting started and maintaining them is going to be a sacrifice for us. But once the habit develops, it will be hard to go a day without them. And the neat thing about this is the more we're crucified with Christ, the more of Christ's joy we're going to experience.[85]

---

84 "Therefore, I tell you, all that you ask for in prayer, believe that you will receive it and it shall be yours" (Mark 11:24).
85 "For as we share abundantly in Christ's sufferings, so through Christ we share abundantly in comfort too" (2 Corinthians 1:5).

Questions for Thought and Discussion

Daily Growing in the Spirit-Filled Life

1. "I have been crucified with Christ; yet I live, no longer I, but Christ lives in me" (Galatians 2:19b–20, NAB). What does this text mean to you personally? How can you apply it to everyday life?

2. How can we crucify our thought life? How can we renew our thought life?

3. How would your life change if your feet were crucified with Jesus's feet on the cross? Or how has your life been changed since your feet were crucified with Jesus's feet on the cross?

4. Have you ever sensed the Holy Spirit calling you to serve in a particular way? Did you respond? What happened?

5. What kind of fellowship are you engaged in right now?

6. What does it mean to share in Trinitarian love?

7. Why is adoration a good place to begin prayer?

8. Give some examples not covered in the book of sins of omission. Why is it important to confess these sins as well as those we actually commit?

9. What are some ways we can cooperate with the Holy Spirit to bring about our own crucifixion?

CHAPTER 13

Daily Experiencing Spiritual Warfare

The Devil Is a Liar

Every day Christians are involved in spiritual warfare whether they're aware of it or not. We know there's a devil out there because he's mentioned in sacred scripture, and it's his job to tempt us to sin. But for the most part, we don't worry a whole lot about him, and he doesn't worry about us.

He doesn't have to. He's influenced the culture we live in, and we just follow its lead. There are probably some who don't even believe the devil exists. This doesn't bother the devil at all. The less people believe in him the easier it is for them to be convinced they are making their own free choices.

But there are several places in the gospels where Jesus encountered the devil.[86] The first instance is when Jesus was tempted by the devil in the wilderness.[87] After this Jesus delivered several people from various symptoms of demonic possession (Luke 4:41). In John 10:18 Jesus said that he saw "Satan fall like lightning from the sky." Jesus was adamant about the existence of the devil.

The devil's reality is even mentioned in the Catechism of the Catholic Church.[88] They are created beings (CCC 391) who have rebelled against God (CCC 392) and strive to destroy God's plan for creation (CCC 395). How is the devil going to do this? By convincing us to turn away from God.

In John 8:44 Jesus tells us the devil "is a liar and the father of lies" (NAB). We can see this from the very beginning when he lied to Eve about eating the forbidden fruit. The devil (characterized as a snake) convinced Eve that God had lied to them, and they would be happiest if they disobeyed his command. It wasn't long after they gave into the devil's temptation they discovered the devil had lied to them.

---

86 See Matthew 4:1–10, Matthew 8:28–34, Mark 3:11, Mark 9:25–26, Luke 4:33–35, Luke 10:18, John 8:44.

87 Matthew 4:1–11 and Luke 4:1–12.

88 See CCC 391, 392, 1237, 1707, 1708, 2851. For more examples see "Demon" in the index of the Catechism.

The same is true with us. God has told us if we follow him and keep his commands we will have an abundant life (John 10:10).[89] But the devil tells us differently. Through the media and culture in general, the devil has convinced many people that God is not powerful enough to make them happy or give them the fulfillment they're seeking. The alternative the devil gives them is any lifestyle that contradicts a relationship with God.

The problem with this is if someone rejects God they're never going to be at peace. They're constantly going to be seeking for more pleasure, more material goods, and more applause to fill their emptiness. And they will experience this emptiness because we have been created for God (CCC 27).

On the other hand, a relationship with God seeks to glorify and serve him alone. We may occasionally struggle with the devil's lies, but God will constantly draw us back to himself.

The best way of fighting against the devil's lies is to counter them with God's promises from scripture. (I have provided a list of sixteen promises for spiritual

---

89 "I came so that they might have life and have it more abundantly."

warfare at the end of the chapter.) The text from John 10:10 [90] and 1 Corinthians 2:9 [91] are good ones for reminding us of God's promise to make us fully happy.

Another lie of the devil's is that God doesn't love us. There are a variety of reasons someone would buy into this lie, but it needs to be countered with God's truth: "For God so loved [your name] that he gave his only Son" (John 3:16). Psalm 139:13–14 is a reminder of how intimately God knows us:

> You formed my inmost being;
> you knit me in my mother's
> womb.
> I praise you because I am
> wonderfully made;
> wonderful are your works!
> My very self you know (NAB).

In Isaiah 49:16 God tells us, "See, upon the palms of my hands I have engraved you" (NAB).

---

90 "A thief come only to steal and slaughter and destroy; I came so that they might have life and have it more abundantly" (NAB).

91 "What no eye has seen, nor ear heard, nor the heart of man conceived, what God has prepared for those who love him" (RSV).

The devil will tell us we're never going to change so we may as well just give in to a life of sin. But Philippians 4:13 tells us that we can do all things through Christ who strengthens us! The devil is also very condemning. Worry over a past or more recent sin will give the devil an open door to start condemning someone. He'll try to convince them that God can't forgive them.

When these thoughts come to us, we can respond with Romans 8:1: "Hence, now there is no condemnation for those who are in Christ Jesus" (NAB). When we sin we need to repent and move on but condemning ourselves is what the devil wants.

Sometimes the devil will catch us in an argument with someone, and he'll give us thoughts that will make us even angrier. We may begin to see the other person as the epitome of evil, increasing our anger towards them. The devil convinces us that they're entirely wrong and there's no way we can ever be reconciled with them. In fact, the devil will convince us that our joy is going to come from being angry.

But Ephesians 6:12 tells us, "For our struggle is not with flesh and blood but with the principalities, with the powers, with the world rulers of this present darkness, with the evil spirits in the heavens" (NAB).

The devil will try to convince us that the enemy is other people when, in fact, he is the true enemy. He is the one trying to destroy us.

At this point, we can either continue listening to the devil's lies, or we can stop and let God take over. If we let God take over then we are making a choice to love. In Matthew 5:44 Jesus tells us to love our enemies, and in John 13:34–35 Jesus said, "I give you a new commandment: love one another. As I have loved you, so you also should love one another" (NAB). The devil's greatest enemy is love.

> Our struggle is not with flesh and blood but ...with the evil spirits in the heavens.

Who Do We Want to Follow?

Every day in a variety of circumstances spiritual warfare is asking us who we want to follow. In Matthew 6:24 we're told: "No one can serve two masters. He will either hate one and love the other or be devoted to one and despise the other" (NAB). Spiritual warfare is about deciding whose side we want to be on.

It seems like this would be an obvious choice, "For the wages of sin is death, but the gift of God is eternal life in Christ Jesus our Lord" (Romans 6:23, NAB). But the reason it's so easy for us to believe the devil's lies is because he makes them sound so attractive to us. Our fallen, carnal nature is drawn to the very things the devil presents to us: sensual pleasure, materialism, self-indulgence, etc. But because we have a free will, we can make a choice not to give in to these temptations.

Whenever a trial comes in our lives, the devil is right there, ready to pounce on us. He tries to convince us that if God really loved us, or if he existed at all, he would not have let this terrible circumstance happen to us. Our natural tendency is to focus on the situation, which will cause us to feel discouraged and depressed. The devil will try to make the situation seem even worse, thereby increasing our bad feelings.

Initially, we're going to want to go with the bad feelings. But as soon as we're aware of them we need to listen to what God has promised us. In Romans 8:28 we're promised that "all things work for good for those who love God" (NAB). And in James 1:2 we are told that trials should be an occasion for pure joy because they help us grow in faith. It's all a matter of looking at the situation through God's eyes.

We need to constantly be leery of the devil's attacks because he "is prowling around like a roaring lion looking for [someone] to devour" (1 Peter 5:8, NAB). As soon as we let down our guard or open ourselves up, he is there for the attack. But once we recognize his attack, we need to be ready with a defense.

In James 4:7 we're told, "Resist the devil and he will flee" (NAB). The more we resist his attacks, the more power we will have over him. That's why it's good to have a plan ahead of time rather than coming up with something after we're already under attack. That's where a familiarity with God's promises comes in.

Weapons of Defense

The best way to maintain a scriptural arsenal of God's promises is to put them to memory. This way the Holy Spirit is able to bring a text to our minds as soon as one is needed. The second-best way is to read and reflect on the text over and over again. This will keep the text in the subconscious, allowing the Holy Spirit to remind us of it when it's needed.

Whether the scriptures are being memorized or not, a different promise can be written on index cards and referred to throughout the day. This will help for both memorization and familiarity. As I mentioned before there are sixteen texts that can be used for this at the end of the chapter. There are actually many more texts that can be used for spiritual warfare, but these are given as a sample. There are many ways one can familiarize themselves with God's promises, but it's important to make them a part of your spiritual arsenal.

The devil is not more powerful than God and we have been given the weapons to fight against him. Indeed, one of the scriptural promises is that "we are more than conquerors through him who loved us" (Romans 8:37, RSV). We already have victory through Jesus Christ. We just have to stand in our victory.

Be Clothed in the Armor of God

A good way of standing in victory is to clothe ourselves everyday with the armor of God. The text this comes from is Ephesians 6:13-17:

Therefore, put on the armor of God, that you may be able to resist on the evil day, having done everything, to hold your ground. Do, stand fast with your loins girded in truth, clothed with righteousness as a breastplate, and your feet shod in readiness for the gospel of peace. In all circumstances, hold faith as a shield, to quench all the flaming arrows of the evil one (NAB).

As soon as we begin the day, we need to realize that we're in a spiritual war zone. We're going to be attacked and we need to be ready for it. Jesus is the center of our lives and our focus needs to be on him, not on the devil.

Still, we need to be ready through whatever means are available to us: prayer, daily Mass, spiritual reading, sacramentals, etc. This will help us to stand our ground against the devil's attacks because it will keep our focus on God. And then we need to put on the armor of protection that God has given us.

In verse 14 we're told to keep our loins girded in truth.

> Keep your loins girded in truth.

St. Paul is referring to the belt that a soldier would clothe himself with. It was the center of his armor, it kept the upper and lower parts together, and it was from the belt that his sword hung. To have his belt girded was to be ready for the fight.

Knowing the promises of God and the teachings of our faith are the truths we need to cling to when defending ourselves against the attacks of the devil. Having this knowledge makes us ready for the fight. Remember that in most cases it will not be our job to attack the devil, but to defend ourselves against his attacks.

Verse 14 also talks about "being clothed with righteousness as a breastplate." The breastplate of armor covered the heart and the internal organs of the soldier. It gave protection to these important areas of the body. Where we get this breastplate of righteousness is through faith in Jesus Christ. We may not always be righteous, but Jesus Christ is.

One of the devil's greatest weapons is to attack us because of our sin, our shortcomings, and our weaknesses. This causes us to feel discouraged and depressed. When the devil attacks us in this way we need to remind ourselves that we are weak, but it's Jesus Christ who has saved us. He is the breastplate of righteousness. As long as we keep ourselves clothed with this knowledge we will be victorious over the devil.

Verse 15 tells us to keep our "feet shod in readiness for the gospel of peace" (NAB). The sandals of a Roman soldier laced up the sides of his legs to give him security in battle. Our spiritual shoes need to make us feel firm in our stand against the evil one.

> Keep your feet shod in readiness.

Often when adversity comes our way we become defeated with a variety of emotions: discouragement, depression, disappointment, anxiety, nervousness, and so on. We're not able to stand firm because we're shaking in our boots.

In John 14:27 Jesus said, "Peace I leave with you; my peace I give to you" (NAB). We must claim that peace and focus on it as much as we can. If we know the truth and have clothed ourselves in Jesus Christ, we should be able to stand on a foundation of peace.

The devil's lie, though, will be that there's no reason to be at peace. He'll have us focus on the situation, blow it out of proportion, and convince us there's no hope at all. It's then that we need to follow St. Paul's warning to us in scripture: "Resist the devil and he will flee from you" (NAB). We need to focus on God's promises and take our focus off the situation.

As we continue to make the choice to do this (because we might not feel like it) we will begin to gain strength over the devil's temptations. We might even want to start praising God and thanking him *for* the situation. We thank him, confident that we are going to see his glory through it.

But if one is still not able to find the peace, they might want to seek additional help. There may, for instance, be a need for the sacrament of reconciliation. There may be the need for professional psychological help. The purpose of this chapter is just to make people aware of the reality of spiritual warfare and some of the basics for dealing with it. Anything beyond that is outside the scope of this chapter.

Verse 16 says, "In all circumstances, hold faith as a shield, to catch all the flaming arrows of the evil one" (NAB). This shield was held by the soldier to give added protection against the arrows of the enemy. This is what our faith in Jesus does. When we're being attacked, the first question we need to ask ourselves is, "Who do I have my faith in? Do I have my faith in my own ability, or is my faith in God?"

> Hold faith as a shield

Proverbs 3:5–6 tells us to trust in the Lord with all our heart and not to rely on our own understanding. We are often going to fail, and others are going to fail us as well. But God will never fail us. In Psalm 23:1 the psalmist says, "The Lord is my shepherd; there is nothing I lack" (NAB). If our faith and our trust is in God, what more do we need?

Verse 17 says, "And take the helmet of salvation." The helmet protects the warrior's brain, the center of his thinking.

> Take the helmet of salvation.

The devil's army is constantly trying to shape our thinking, or to change the way we look at things. His goal is to convince us that everything we have been taught about goodness and holiness is wrong and should be shunned. What is right are those things that we had previously been taught to be wrong. It's like the people Isaiah was speaking to when he said:

> Ah! Those who call evil good
> and good evil,
> who change darkness to
> light, and light into
> darkness,
> who change bitter to sweet
> and sweet to bitter!
> (Isaiah 5:20, NAB)

Through media, social pressure, advertisement, entertainment and so on, we are told that Christian values were for a former time. Since they are not in sync with contemporary, progressive thinking they need to be avoided and discouraged. We need to fill our minds with the word of God.

Verse 17 also tells us the word of God is the sword of the Spirit. This is what we use to fight against the attacks on our faith and values. We use this knowledge to give an answer to others, but even more to fight against the attacks of the devil on our minds.

> The sword of the Spirit is the word of God.

Some people like to check their spiritual armor in the morning when they pray. They read the text and reflect on the presence of each armor part in their arsenal for the day. Is everything in its place? Are my loins girded in truth? Am I clothed with the breastplate of righteousness? Am I holding faith as a shield against the flaming arrows of the evil one? Have I put on the helmet of salvation by becoming familiar with the word of God? Am I learning how to use God's word to fight against spiritual attacks?

Every day we need to be ready for the devil's attacks because we are in a spiritual war zone. The only way we're going to survive is by learning how to use some of the weapons God has given us.

Questions for Thought and Discussion

Daily Experiencing Spiritual Warfare

1. Before this teaching, were you aware that you're living in a spiritual war zone?

2. Can you think of a time that you've been spiritually attacked? If it's not too personal can you share this with the group?

3. In what ways can you see the devil trying to influence the cultural thinking of today?

4. How can the devil influence someone's thinking in an argument? Can you give a scripture to counter the devil's argument?

5. Can you give an example of the devil lying to our culture? What are the consequences of this lie?

6. What are some things we can do to gird our loins in truth?

7. How can we keep our feet shod for the gospel of peace?

8. Give some examples of the flaming arrows of the evil one. How does faith function as a shield against these?

9. Do you think most people in our culture believe in the devil? What do they think he's like? Do they think we should be concerned about him? Why do you think they believe this way?

CHAPTER 14

Sixteen Scriptural Promises for Spiritual Warfare

1. "Take delight in the Lord and he will give you the desires of your heart" (Psalm 37:4, RSV).

2. "I can do all things through him who strengthens me" (Philippians 4:13, RSV).

3. "I have said this to you, that in me you may have peace. In the world you will have tribulation; but be of good cheer. I have overcome the world" (John 16:33, RSV).

4. "But whoever drinks the water I shall give will never thirst; the water I shall give will become in him a spring of water welling up to eternal life" (John 4:14, NAB).

5. "Weeping may tarry for the night, but joy comes with the morning" (Psalm 30:5, RSV).

6. "And behold, I am with you always, until the end of the age" (Matthew 28:20, NAB).

7. "He will wipe every tear from their eye, and there will be no more death or mourning, wailing or pain, for the old order has passed away" (Revelation 21:4, NAB).

8. Are not two sparrows sold for a small coin? Yet not one of them falls to the ground without your Father's knowledge. Even all the hairs on your head are counted. So, do not be afraid; you are worth more than many sparrows" (Matthew 10:29–31, NAB).

9. "So do not worry and say, 'What are we to eat?' or 'What are we to wear?' All these things the pagans seek. Your heavenly Father knows that you need them all. But seek first the kingdom of God and his righteousness, and all these things will be given you besides" (Matthew 7:31–33, NAB).

10. "A thief comes only to steal and slaughter and destroy; I came so that they [you] might have life and have it more abundantly" (John 10:10, NAB).

11. "Behold, I stand at the door and knock. If anyone hears my voice and opens the door, I will enter his house and dine with him, and he with me" (Revelation 4:20, NAB).

12. "Can a mother forget her infant, be without tenderness for the child of her womb? Even should she forget, I will never forget you. See, upon the palms of my hands I have engraved you" (Isaiah 49:15–16, NAB).

13. "And whatever you ask in my name, I will do, so that the Father may be glorified in the Son. If you ask anything of me in my name, I will do it" (John 14:12–14, NAB).

14. "We know that in everything God works for good with those who love him" (Romans 8:28, RSV).

15. "Who shall separate us from the love of Christ? Shall tribulation, or distress or distress, or persecution, or famine, or nakedness, or peril, or sword? . . . No, in all these things we are more than conquerors through him who loved us. For I am sure that neither death, nor life, nor angels, nor principalities, nor things present, nor things to come, nor powers, nor height, nor death, nor

anything else in all creation, will be able to separate us from the love of God I Christ Jesus our Lord" (Romans 8:35 & 37–39, RSV).

16. "Why are you downcast, my soul; why do you groan within me? Wait for God, for I shall again praise him, my savior and my God" (Psalm 42:6 & 12.)

CHAPTER 15

The Invitation

This is an invitation for you to discover and use the gifts God has given you. When we think of the word "gift" we often imagine someone who is very gifted in a certain area. Gifted musicians, singers, actors, teachers, surgeons, preachers, mathematicians, scientists, and so on are people we think of as being at the top of their field. This is not what it means to have a gift of the Holy Spirit. A gift of the Holy Spirit is the power of the Holy Spirit working through us.

It doesn't matter whether we have anything to give or not. What matters is what God has to give through us. The classic story from scripture is from John 6:1–15. Jesus asked Philip where they could get enough food to feed the five thousand men (to say nothing of the women and children) who had gathered to hear him teach.

Philip was astonished that Jesus would even make such a request and said, "Two hundred days' wages worth of food would not be enough for each of them to have a little [bit]" (NAB). Then it was discovered that a young boy had five loaves of bread and two fish.

The boy apparently gave these to Jesus, and Jesus blessed and used them to feed the multitude. In the same way, when we give Jesus the seemingly small gift that we might have he can use that to do miraculous things too. But it helps to know that we have a gift to give to Jesus.

Throughout this book on the L.I.G.H.T. seminar we've gone over some of the gifts of the Holy Spirit and their use in everyday life. We've discussed the holiness gifts of Isaiah 11:2–3: wisdom, understanding, counsel, fortitude, knowledge, piety, and fear of the Lord. There were the word gifts: tongues, the interpretation of tongues, and teaching.

The gifts of power included miracles and healing. Prophecy, the word of knowledge, and mental images were mentioned with the revelation gifts. There are the gifts of service and the gifts from Ephesians 4:11: apostleship, evangelization, and pastoring. These aren't all the gifts of the Holy Spirit but are some that any one of us might have. The important thing is to pray about it and serve. As you continue to serve and grow in sensitivity to the Holy Spirit you will see God's gifts begin to work through you.

On May 30 of 1998 Saint Pope John Paul II gave a speech to nearly a million people involved with ecclesial movements and new ministries. At one point in the speech he said,

> Today, I would like to cry out to all of you gathered here in St Peter's Square and to all Christians: open yourselves docilely to the gifts of the Spirit! Accept gratefully and obediently the charisms which the Spirit never ceases to bestow on us! Do not forget that every charism is given for the common good—that is, for the benefit of the whole Church.[92]

Our task as Catholic Christians is to use the gifts God has given us to continue Jesus's ministry on earth. The whole world is hungering to meet Jesus and our job is to bring Jesus to them. One of the ways God has prepared for us to do this is through the gifts of the Holy Spirit.

---

92 Pope John Paull II, "For the World Congress of Ecclesial Movements and New Communities," (May 30, 1998), Vatican website.

CHAPTER 16

Prayer to the Holy Spirit

O, Holy Spirit, grant that I may be sensitive to your guidance. Grant me the wisdom to see those things you want me to do, and the courage to do them. Show me the gifts I have been given, enabling me to serve you through serving others. Use me as a source of bringing your miracles, your love, your healing, your peace, your hope, your joy, and your new life to others. Pour forth a fountain of living water within me so that I can share your living water with others. In Jesus's name. Amen

Bibliography

Augustine, St. *The City of God.* Translated by Gerald G. Walsh, S.J., Demetrius B. Zema, S.J., Grace Monahah, O.S.U., Daniel J. Honan. New York: Doubleday, 1958.

Bennett, Dennis J. *Nine O'Clock in the Morning.* Alachua: BridgeLogos, 1970.

Catechism of the Catholic Church 2nd ed. United States Catholic Conference of Bishops. The Holy See: Librereia Editrice Vaticana, 2000.

Cieszinski, Joseph D. *Loaves and Fishes: Jesus and the Feeding of the Multitudes. Multiplication Stories of the Bible and the Church and Their Relevance Today.* Goleta: Queenship, 2016.

Collected Works of St. John of the Cross. Translated by Kieran Kavanaugh, OCD and Otilio Rodriguez, OCD. Washington, D.C.: Institute of Carmelite Studies, 1979.

Collected Works of St. Teresa of Avila, Vol. 2. Translated by Kieran Kavanaugh, OCD and Otilio Rodriguez, OCD. Washington, D.C.: Institute of Carmelite Studies, 1980.

Congar, Yves. *I Believe in the Holy Spirit.* Translated by David Smith. New York: Herder Crossroad, 2005.

Dulles, Avery, S.J. *Models of the Church.* New York: Doubleday, 1987.

Ensley, Eddie. *Sounds of Wonder: A Popular History of Speaking in Tongues in the Catholic Tradition.* New York/Ramsey: Paulist Press, 1977.

Flannery, Austin, ed., *Vatican Council II: The Conciliar and Postconciliar Documents.* Collegeville: Liturgical Press, 1996.

Francis I. "Address to the Renewal in the Holy Spirit Movement," St. Peter's Square, Friday, July 3, 2015. The Holy See: Libreria Editrice Vaticana. Vatican website.

Gallagher-Mansfield, Patti. *As by A New Pentecost.* Steubenville: Franciscan University Press, 1992.

John XXIII. *Humanae Salutis,* #23. Dec. 25, 1961. The Holy See: Libreria Editrice Vaticana. Vatican website.

John Paul II. "Message of Pope John Paul II for the Wolrd Congress of Ecclesial Movements and New

Communities," Saturday, 30 May 1998. The Holy See: Libreria Editrice Vaticana. Vatican website.

Kolodiejchuk, Brian, ed., *Mother Teresa: Come Be My Light: The Private Writings of the "Saint of Calcutta."* New York: Doubleday, 2007.

Life in the Spirit Seminars Team Manual Catholic Edition. Developed by the Word of God. Ann Arbor: Servant Books, 1979.

Linguistic Society of America. "How Many Languages Are There in the World?" https://www.linguisticsociety. org/content/how-manylanguages-are-there-world

McDonnell, Kilian, and Montague, George T. *Christian Initiation and Baptism in the Holy Spirit: Evidence from the First Eight Centuries.* Collegeville: The Liturgical Press, 1994.

National Directory for Catechesis. United States Conference of Catholic Bishops, Washington, D.C., 2005.

Paul VI. "Salvifici Doloris: On the Christian Meaning of Human Suffering, 1984." The Holy See: Libreria Editrice Vaticana. Vatican website.

Pius X. *Vehementer Nos: On the French Law of Separation*, #8, Feb.11, 1906. The Holy See: Libreria Editrice Vaticana. Vatican website.

Rite of Christian Initiation of Adults. National Conference of Catholic Bishops. New York: Catholic Book Publishing Co., 1988

Puhl, Luis J. S.J., trans. and ed., *Spiritual Exercises of St. Ignatius of Loyola.* Chicago: Loyola University Press, 1951.

Suenens, Joseph Léon. *A New Pentecost?* New York: Seabury Press, 1975.

About the Author

Deacon Michael Wesley was born in Los Angeles, California, but has lived most of his life in Albuquerque, New Mexico. He graduated from the University of New Mexico with a Bachelor of Science degree in education, and a Master of Arts degree in special education. In 2003 he was ordained to the Permanent Diaconate for the Archdiocese of Santa Fe, and in 2009 he received a Master of Theological Studies degree from St. Norbert's College.

Deacon Mike and his wife, Kathy, are coleaders of Souls on Fire, a prayer group that meets at the Catholic Charismatic Center in Albuquerque. Deacon Mike ministers as a deacon at St. Therese of the Infant Jesus Parish. He coordinates the adult RCIA, leads a Bible study, and participates in liturgy. He mentors a group of men who are in formation for the diaconate along with their wives, and he facilitates online classes in theology for the virtual learning center at Dayton University. He also teaches courses in theology through the Archdiocese of Santa Fe.

Deacon Mike and Kathy host a radio program for

the Catholic radio station in their area called *Deacons Alive*. Once a month they interview deacons and their wives, discussing the various ministries of the diaconate.

Deacon Mike is a cradle Catholic who attended Catholic school from the first through the eighth grade. Due to his parent's divorce his family stopped attending Mass when he was fourteen years old. At age nineteen, however, a conversion experience drew him back into the Catholic Church. That was in 1971.

Since then, the desire of his heart has been to help others meet Jesus as the one who loves them and can give them an abundant life. His prayer is that this book, and the LIGHT seminar, will help its readers and participants discover the gifts God has given them, and the freedom to use these gifts in everyday life.

CPSIA information can be obtained
at www.ICGtesting.com
Printed in the USA
LVHW051015070121
675504LV00006B/465